AN
OPEN
ADOPTION

AN
OPEN
ADOPTION

Lincoln Caplan

Houghton Mifflin Company

BOSTON

Library of Congress Cataloging-in-Publication Data
Caplan, Lincoln.
An open adoption / Lincoln Caplan.
p.   cm.
Originally published: New York : Farrar, Straus & Giroux, 1990.
Includes bibliographical references.
ISBN 0-395-58669-0
1. Adoption — United States — Psychological aspects — Case studies.
I. Title.
HV875.55.C37   1991   91-6310
362.7′34′0973 — dc20   CIP

Printed in the United States of America

BP 10 9 8 7 6 5 4 3 2 1

Published by arrangement with Farrar, Straus & Giroux.

Most of this book originally appeared in *The New Yorker*.

This edition includes editorial revisions made by the author
after the original hardcover publication.

For SLC and MSC

Contents

AN
OPEN
ADOPTION

Author's Note

The following is an account of an open adoption that raises central questions about adoption in America today. Like many drawn to write about the subject, I am personally involved in adoption—in my case, as an adoptive father. I hope this interest has sharpened, rather than biased, my awareness and judgment.

When I began to report about the adoption described here, in the summer of 1988, each of the four adults integrally involved made a commitment to give me his or her full cooperation, on the condition that I change their names and those of some others in my writing, along with some other identifying details, to protect their privacy, while presenting the essential truth of the story. I have abided by that agreement. Each of the four adults gave permission to employees of the Jewish Family Service of Greater Framingham, in Massachusetts, and of the law offices of Diane Michelsen, in Walnut Creek, California, to speak with me about the adoption. The birth mother and the adoptive parents also encouraged me to speak with the midwife and nurse who presided at the birth, which I did.

The subject of adoption has received more public attention

in the past few years than at any previous time. Too often, what has been written does not reflect the fundamental changes in the adoption process that have evolved in the past decade and a half. Much of the coverage is still shaped by a sentiment expressed in *Peter Pan*. At the end of the play, the Darling children return from Never-Never Land with some of the Lost Boys. Mr. Darling's blithe agreement to take the boys into the household depicts adoption as offering a carefree future to parentless children who have no past. The institution was never that simple, and its story has never been more unpredictable than it is today.

Premonitions

In early June of 1988, Margaret Bass decided to place the baby she was expecting for adoption. She was six and a half months pregnant, twenty years old, and a junior at the University of Delaware, near Wilmington. The baby's father and Peggy's boyfriend (she was rarely called Margaret) was Thomas Spaeth, a recent Delaware graduate, who was twenty-two. Tom and Peggy had been together for almost two years. They first got involved when Tom brought some wine coolers to a party during the summer of 1986 and went to stash the jugs in a room where Peggy was sleeping. He woke her up. Peggy didn't have her glasses on and couldn't focus on him. Tom said not long ago: "For the first time since I had known her, she looked cute. Because she couldn't see me. One thing she'll do if she can see you is she'll pin you with a gaze."

Peggy was a marketing major, with a minor in music. (She was a light soprano.) Tom's degree was in music (he played the guitar), and he hoped to become a studio engineer for rock musicians. By the fall of 1987, they had decided they were in love and had begun to discuss marriage. But Tom was in no rush, and Peggy had no need to push him. They both planned to start careers, make some money, have fun. After his graduation in the spring of that year, Tom had put off looking for a job so he could play for a while. When he settled down to search, it was the slow season in the Wilmington–Philadelphia audio business (the cities are thirty miles apart), and jobs were scarce. "I was unemployed, though I freelanced, doing music videos for some groups," he said. "I have a lot of talent and ability at what I do, but I didn't have what you need, which is job experience."

Peggy considered the pregnancy her problem. She didn't tell her family, with whom she lived in Wilmington, because she was afraid the news would upset them too much. She was also sure they would insist on helping her keep the baby. ("My whole family is baby-crazy," Peggy said. "Babies must live in fear of us, because we swoop down and chubby-cheek them until their faces fall off.") The precariousness of her family's finances (her father is a potter and a dealer in model ships, and her mother makes clothing for children's dolls) and of her parents' marriage (they were considering divorce), she said, convinced her that keeping the baby would be in nobody's interest.

For a time, Peggy had also withheld the news from Tom. She tried to break up with him or to goad him into breaking up with her. Neither approach worked, and eventually Peggy told Tom she was having some physical problems and needed to spend some time with him. He suggested that they take a room at a Ramada Inn for the weekend, and the following Monday, still not knowing, Tom escorted her to see a doctor. The appointment was for a sonogram to check on the progress of the fetus.

By early June, Peggy was dressing to hide her pregnancy (blouses with big shoulder pads, belts slung on her hips), in what she called conscious "fashion mistakes." She tried to walk as if she weren't pregnant (pelvis and hips tilted back). She ate most of her meals at restaurants or at the university cafeteria, and skimped at home, where, because she looked plump, her mother had put her on a diet. But the curve of her belly was making her feel that she needed to get out of town soon, before her family really noticed. One Sunday, she was leafing through the want ads of the Camden *Courier-Post*, published in New Jersey, looking for a job in that area for Tom, she said, and noticed an ad:

ADOPTION—We are a happily married, financially secure couple hoping to share our love, our lives and our future with an infant. If you are considering adoption, please let us be part of it. Confidential, expenses paid. Please call our attorney collect.

A California number was listed. The ad appealed to Peggy. It didn't specify a white infant, though Peggy and Tom are white, or a healthy one, though Peggy had confidence in the fetus she was carrying; the ad seemed to extend a kind hand rather than a grasping one. She wrote down the phone number, and the following Friday she called at lunchtime (around nine o'clock in the morning in California). A young woman answered and accepted the charges. Jumping right in, Peggy explained that she was pregnant, couldn't keep the baby, and wanted to find a couple to adopt it. The young woman said, "That's the most wonderful thing I've ever heard!" Peggy said later: "Boom! Right off the bat! To have them say that to me— I was just, like, *somebody* understands what I'm asking."

In a version of their story which Peggy related about four months after her call to California and which Tom initially supported, she and Tom had conceived the baby when they made love to celebrate her twentieth birthday, on November 23, 1987. Several weeks later, Peggy said, a doctor confirmed for her what she had figured. "You always read about the woman who wakes up and thinks, I'm pregnant," Peggy commented. "It wasn't quite that way. It was more like, Maybe something's wrong. Despite the best methods of birth control, somehow a sperm got through all that."

When Tom found out about the pregnancy, sometime in February, he was shocked ("My first reaction was a big, looming fear of hell") and angry ("I got mad at the world for throwing a monkey wrench into the love that we had"), but he made an effort to be consoling. "There was a lot of pain," Tom said, supporting Peggy's story. "She didn't want to put me through this, because she felt that I had a lot of dreams and a lot of wants and a lot of needs, and that all of this might destroy some of what makes me good at what I do and happy at what I do."

They agreed not to tell anyone they knew, and especially not to tell their families. Tom's mother was a prosperous insurance agent and his father a senior parks administrator, and having achieved their own financial comfort (which they generously shared with him even as an adult—they gave Tom a new silver Volkswagen Rabbit, and the family's vacation house, at Rehoboth Beach, was in his name, he said), they had high expectations for him as well. "My family, sooner or later, would have reacted with love and understanding," Tom said. "But there would have been a price to pay." Peggy: "The reason we couldn't tell anybody is that everyone would have encouraged us to keep the baby."

For the next several months, according to Peggy's story, Peggy and Tom went about their business. The pregnancy seemed to be going well, but Peggy took no steps toward giving up the baby: she wanted to wait until she was certain the pregnancy was trouble-free, she explained. She had been seeing a doctor about once a month (each time, she said, she saw a different doctor and made up a new name for herself), and after four and a half months she was assured that the fetus was flourishing.

Peggy was always certain of her intentions. "I never entertained the thought of not having the baby, nor did I entertain the thought of marriage," she said later. "I just knew in my heart that if God intended me to be married and have this baby, then that would have happened." She began to read about adoption and to develop ideas about the kind of adoption she wanted. She liked the sound of a semi-open adoption, in which a lawyer or an agency would help her find a couple waiting to adopt. They would select each other, although the information used to make the match could be generic ("the birth mother is a twenty-year-old college junior majoring in marketing and music"), and the adults might never meet. This contrasted with what she thought of as traditional adoption, in which she would turn the baby over to an adoption agency and the agency would decide where to place the child—in an old-fashioned example, by assigning the baby to the couple next in line on the agency's waiting list. Some traditional agencies had separate doors for pregnant women and potential adopters, she had heard, to keep them from meeting even by chance.

To Peggy, semi-open adoption made sense, because she could "know where the baby was going," the adopting parents could "know where the baby was coming from," and the baby could eventually know that it was loved—by the adopting parents (Peggy called them Mom and Dad) but also by her. A review of the experiences Tom had heard about from his adopted friends led him, too, to think that semi-open adoption was the better option. Those adoptees, who came from traditional adoptions, didn't know who their original, or birth, parents were. They either thought "low of themselves" because they believed that they weren't wanted or had convinced themselves "there was some terrible accident" that had led to their adoptions. To Tom, these friends had "spent their entire lives not doing what they were meant to do but looking for whoever they'd come from."

Peggy said, when she first related what had happened, that she had got in touch with two adoption agencies. The first was a private agency located in the South. She phoned and found the woman she spoke with to be "nice, but rather ambiguous about some basics." When Peggy said she wanted to know about the couple who would be her baby's adoptive parents and wanted them to know about her, the woman hedged. Peggy: "I felt like, if they're hedging now they're going to *really* hedge when I tell them I have to move out of state to have this baby."

The second agency was a Catholic Charities not far from Wilmington. Peggy described herself to them as a "semi-scheduled Episcopalian," meaning that she went to church occasionally. Tom, however, had been brought up Catholic, and although he did not accept certain Church dogmas (he believed in abortion and described the Pope as a "fool" about birth control), he still identified with the Church. Peggy visited the agency for an interview. Instead of a gratifying welcome, she said, she was given a lecture on religion and morality.

"I kept stressing, 'We're in love, we're going to get married,' " Peggy recounted. "So they said, 'Well, if he's a good Catholic, why isn't he marrying you?' " Peggy went on: "Catholic Charities would just give you a brief file, no other information, nothing. I didn't know if the baby was going to a loving couple. I mean, I'm sure the agency screened people, but my grandmother, before she retired, was a social worker, and I heard stories about children being placed with a couple that had been approved by social workers and then, all of a sudden, something terrible was wrong, and they end up being weirdos and not being able to care for the child. And that whole thing up in New York"—the highly publicized case in which Lisa Steinberg, a six-year-old girl who had been adopted illegally, was beaten to death by her "adoptive" father— "really, really affected how I was thinking. That was a bad, bad time."

In a second version of their story, which Tom told nearly a year after Peggy found the ad in the paper, she had had no early intuition about her pregnancy. She discovered it only after four months, not several weeks. Rather than learning about the pregnancy at two and a half months, Tom found out about it at six and a half. Tom: "People say, 'You were sleeping with this person and you didn't know she was six and a half months pregnant?' There were little things that were different. She wanted the lights out all the time. She acted weird sometimes. But she did a good job on me and her family."

Peggy didn't entertain the thought of aborting her pregnancy because she was too far along when she discovered it, he surmised, but she probably thought a lot about marriage: he asked her to marry him after she had shared her secret. Tom: "I said, 'That's it. We'll have to get married.' I think she thought I didn't want it that much. At that point, I didn't. She said, 'No, I'm going to give the child away.' " When they learned, even later, about the pregnancy, Tom's family concluded that Peggy had got pregnant on purpose, to force him to marry her, he said.

The picture of the pregnancy became blurred only much later. Tom described one key moment for him consistently. Late on Monday night, after learning about the pregnancy over the weekend, Tom said, he was driving home and stopped to put some gasoline in his car. "To say from this weekend that I was drained is an understatement," he said later. "I'm pumping gas into my car, at a station on a corner. There's nothing around this station. There's some buildings across the street, and the station is just a station, with a little snack shop inside. White fluorescent light and the dark. I'm pumping gas and I look up and there's a girl walking on the sidewalk next to me. She's got black shoes on, gray pants, and a gray top, and dark hair, and dark eyes like mine, and she's tall, and she's just walking along the road, and I'm looking at her as I'm pumping gas and I think the classic, Gee, she'll see me looking at her so I'd better look down, so I looked down, and when I looked up again she was gone. Not there at all. I didn't hear any footsteps. I didn't hear any running. I dropped the pump and ran over to where she'd been. I ran across the street. The gas-station attendant must have thought I went wild. I ran up to him and said, 'Did you see a woman there?' He said, 'No, I didn't see anything.' Something in my head said, 'That's my daughter when she's grown up.' "

Species Recognition

The ad that had caught Peggy's attention in the New Jersey paper actually represented an inquiry on behalf of six couples. Including Peggy's call, the ad drew ten responses. It had cost approximately a hundred dollars to run for seven days in the paper, and had been placed by a California lawyer named Diane Michelsen. Michelsen had worked as an adoption social worker for Los Angeles County and for the state of California, and as an adviser about foster care to the mayor of San Francisco, before taking a break to renovate houses and go to Golden Gate Law School. In 1981, when she was thirty-five, she set up her own general law practice in San Francisco. Within a couple of years, she was working full-time on adoptions. In California, eighty percent of all adoptions are arranged by lawyers independently of agencies. In many of these adoptions, the pregnant woman (the birth mother) or, infrequently, both the woman and her sexual partner (the birth parents) choose and know the names of the prospective adopters (the adoptive parents). Almost all the adoptions that Michelsen helps arrange involve a meeting between the birth mother and the adoptive couple; three-fourths involve some continuing contact between them, through exchanges of pictures and letters; and about ten percent lead to continuing relationships through phone calls and visits back and forth.

Michelsen helps arrange about ninety adoptions a year. Many of the pregnant women who get in touch with her office learn about her through ads she runs in the Yellow Pages in California, speeches she gives, and articles she writes, or through the network of lawyers, psychologists, social workers, and others who know about her practice.

About forty percent of Michelsen's inquiries from potential birth mothers come in response to newspaper ads like the one Peggy saw. She tries to advertise in communities where there are people who look like the couples on whose behalf she's advertising: for a set of tall, Scandinavian-looking couples she would advertise in Washington State, Minnesota, and Wisconsin. She also advertises in papers serving cities with colleges or where unemployment is high, and tries to place ads where clients ask her to. She observes limits: she won't take an ad in a Texas paper during the tornado season when people are distracted, for example; and there are eighteen states where newspaper advertising like hers is illegal. The ads that she takes in *USA Today* draw the highest number of responses (about thirty for a five-day ad that costs a thousand dollars), but a relatively high percentage of the responses lead nowhere. The ads she places in small, local papers (the Camden *Courier-Post*, circulation 104,000; the *Tribune Review* in Greensburg, Pennsylvania, circulation 55,000; the Woonsocket *Call*, in Rhode Island, circulation 30,000) are cheaper and usually more effective.

When a pregnant woman responds to an ad, Michelsen or another lawyer in the office tries to counsel her generally. The message is: We're going to give you choices, and time to make them. What you are thinking of doing might be right for you, or it might not. If you place your baby for adoption, it will be the hardest thing you have ever done. Michelsen explains the legal process of adoption, gathers information about the health, ethnic background, and social history of the woman and, if possible, her sexual partner (including information about any drug use or exposure to AIDS), and tries to assess the birth mother's level of commitment to adoption. If Michelsen decides that the woman is a good prospect—is serious about adoption, understands what's at stake, is healthy, and isn't shopping around among adoption agencies and lawyers— she offers the woman help in qualifying for medical insurance, in figuring out how she can cover the other costs of her pregnancy, and in finding potential parents for the baby. Michelsen doesn't charge birth mothers for this service; it is the prospective adoptive parents who pay the fees (in 1989, $240 per hour) that cover her costs in counseling them and the birth mothers and yield her practice a profit.

Michelsen presents prospective adopters to potential birth mothers through résumés. She asks prospective adopters to imagine that they are writing an order for the perfect birth parents for their child (Where do they live? How old are they? What do they do?) and then to tell her about their fantasies. Then she asks the prospective adopters to describe themselves in terms that might appeal to their ideal birth parents, in a letter no longer than seven paragraphs. Michelsen has the prospective adopters print up their letter on colored paper and submit it with pictures. She has strong views about this package. Green paper doesn't work well as a background—it can make people in the accompanying snapshots look green. Dark-blue paper has a sad cast. Bright colors (yellows, buffs, some mauves, some blues) are cheery and usually successful. The best pictures capture people in warm, unguarded moments and suggest that they have room in their lives for a child. Michelsen believes that couples shouldn't use photographs in which they appear too wrapped up in themselves.

A typical Michelsen file contains résumés mostly of white, middle-aged, home-owning, pet-loving, heterosexual, financially secure California couples. Couples list their adoption counselors and tell about the extended families that await their babies. Among the less conventional prospective adopters was a white pediatrician who was already a single father to six children of different races, ranging from a seventeen-year-old South American Indian boy to an eighteen-month-old black girl, and who reported that the "older children were ecstatic and helpful when the newborns arrived at home." A prospective single mother wrote that she had "undivided attention" to give a baby. (She volunteered, "I am not married now but I would choose to adopt even if I were. It is a choice I have known I would make since my experiences as a birth mother.") Two gay men, who had been together for eleven years, indicated, "Although the picture may not express it, we are an amazingly traditional couple!" The couple with the least fancy jobs were the manager and the assistant manager of a minimart. One couple included a deaf woman. Another had lost their first adopted baby at fourteen months; his heart became diseased soon after he was born, and his body had rejected a transplant.

A young lawyer named Elizabeth Rice took Peggy's call. She found Peggy intelligent and self-confident and thought her self-awareness was impressive. She told Peggy briefly about the six couples represented by the *Courier-Post* ad, and Peggy asked her to read the résumés for three. The third was a Massachusetts couple identified as Daniel and Lee Stone. (Lee's legal surname is Duncan.) The first paragraph of their letter said, "We would like to introduce ourselves and let you know of our deep desire to adopt a baby. We are in our late thirties and have known each other for seven years. On the first night we met in Boston we discovered that we were both born in the same hospital in Denver, Colorado. It was nice to learn that even as infants we had lived under the same roof. We were married in 1984, are very happy together, and want very much to have a family." And the last paragraph said, "We can only imagine how difficult it must be to make the decision to give up your baby. But if there is any comfort to be had from this decision, we want to assure you that we will do everything in our power to give him or her the most wonderful home in the world." In between, they related that Dan taught botany at the Massachusetts Institute of Technology, that Lee had worked as a teacher in a day-care program and as a prenatal nurse and collected children's books, and that they both liked music, sports, and animals, especially their marmalade cat named Otis. Attached to the résumé was a picture of Otis snoozing in the sun.

Peggy couldn't see what the package looked like (buff paper, burnt-orange lettering, and pictures of Otis and the Stones), but Elizabeth Rice read the text to her over the phone. Peggy thought: She's a nurse. He's a botany professor at MIT. Elizabeth said they have a wonderful sense of humor. They have a cat. That's *them.* Peggy asked Rice to call the Stones right away and say she was eager to speak with them.

Rice got off the phone and consulted with Michelsen. Peggy had presented a strong case about her adoption plans and said she needed to move away from home soon, so they decided to telescope the steps they usually follow with birth mothers. They would send Peggy materials from the three couples she had first been interested in and, in the meantime, call the Stones to see if they wanted Peggy to phone them. (In Michelsen's practice, it is more often prospective adopters who decide against pursuing a lead with a potential birth mother than the other way around.) They were charmed by the message Peggy asked Rice to pass along. She had said, "Tell them I'm carrying their baby!"

Lee had suffered a miscarriage on a delayed honeymoon trip in Portugal, in May of 1985. Of that pregnancy, she said recently, "I always knew something was wrong, because I felt so great." She miscarried again in 1986. Although it is common to wait for three miscarriages before testing to see if the cause is a genetic abnormality, Lee and Dan had a workup done on a sample of tissue from the second fetus. Lee: "It was a girl. The genetic abnormality was on the twenty-third chromosome. That's pretty amazing, having a photograph of this fetus's chromosomes."

By then, Lee was thirty-eight years old. (Dan was thirty-six.) Her doctor found that her ovaries were failing. He decided to try boosting her chances of conceiving again by giving her Pergonal, a drug often prescribed to stimulate the growth of ovarian follicles from which an egg might develop. Seven to ten evenings a month, Dan injected her with the drug. On those days, Lee stopped by the hospital so the doctor could check on the growth of her follicles with a sonogram. When a follicle or two looked ready to produce, a nurse injected her with another drug, called HCG (human chorionic gonadotropin), a hormone that stimulates the ovaries and can yield an egg. Lee and Dan then had thirty to thirty-six hours within which to have intercourse and try to conceive.

For a year after beginning the Pergonal treatment, Lee and Dan failed to conceive. Lee grew increasingly depressed about their infertility. She quit her nursing job after it became too painful for her to see women coming back to the hospital to have second and third children, when she couldn't have one. She and Dan stopped seeing close friends with children: they reminded Lee too acutely of her loss. She joined an experimental program at a hospital in Boston (she called it her "mind-body group") that was designed to teach women with fertility problems to meditate in order to reduce stress and perhaps to increase their chances of getting pregnant. Dan also floundered. Lee persuaded him to join her in therapy with Rochelle Friedman, a psychiatrist specializing in infertility, and, with Bonnie Gradstein, the co-author of a book called *Surviving Pregnancy Loss*.

One of Friedman's tenets is that no one ever fully resolves his or her grief about infertility. Resolution involves a process of working, and reworking, through the anguish and loss of not being able to conceive and give birth to a child. For women, infertility can cause problems of great urgency, because so many derive their self-esteem from the capacity to fill a maternal role. For men, too, infertility can lead to a bleak and pervasive sense of loss, though they are reluctant to accept its finality and to move on to considering other ways of having a family. For infertile couples, in Friedman's view, adoption is no panacea. It is initially a safety net for people who have lost hope; it can become a door through which couples pass to gain some control over circumstances that have made them feel powerless and joyless.

Lee and Dan warmed to the prospect of adoption at different rates. By the fall of 1987, after two miscarriages, Lee felt ready. Dan did not. Some of his reluctance stemmed from stories they had heard about couples waiting for five years to adopt through public agencies, and a year or two through private ones. In September, however, some close friends of theirs, Jim and Dina Rose, who had been unable to conceive, adopted a baby boy they named Jacob. After several years of in-vitro fertilization treatments to get Dina pregnant, the Roses had adopted through a conventional private agency. They didn't know anyone who had done otherwise, and had explored no other adoption options. Lee's tense response to meeting Jacob persuaded Dan that they had to do something for themselves about adoption.

They had heard about a Colombian agency called the Instituto Colombiano de Bienestar Familiar, which places Colombian children with Americans. In 1987, 724 Colombian children were adopted in the United States, ranking that country third behind Korea (5,910) and India (807) as the place of origin for foreign-born adoptees. They counted up the reasons for applying and sent a letter to the agency. They liked the notion of adopting a Latin-American baby. They both spoke Spanish and had a special feeling for Latin America. Lee had majored in Latin-American history in college and had spent a year as a rescue nurse in Guatemala after a major earthquake struck the country. Dan had visited Central America regularly, as a tourist and a botanist. To adopt a Hispanic baby, where there was no question that the child was adopted, appealed to him especially: it would make something that was true obviously true—there would be no way to pretend otherwise.

Three weeks later, they received a reply. Among other things, the institute asked for letters from their clergyman and local police vouching for their good character and their intentions about adoption. It advised that any Colombian baby that they adopted might have been born with complications from the birth mother's malnourishment. It also said that they both had to be under thirty-seven to adopt through the agency. That ruled them out. Lee: "I saw all this and realized there was no guarantee we were going to get a healthy baby. I didn't feel strong enough to take on that big possibility." Dan: "It started being something else besides our becoming parents, some other kind of commitment that I wasn't sure I wanted to make. We didn't really know what our options were. You stick your foot in somewhere, and that's where we stuck it in."

Not long after, the Stones learned about the Jewish Family Service, of Framingham, Massachusetts, a small, nonsectarian agency not far from where they lived, whose adoption program was run by Paul Dubroff. He had previously worked for many years for the Jewish Family and Children's Service of Boston and in the late seventies had helped write new rules about adoptions in Massachusetts. Lee and Dan went to see Dubroff in October. He told them, "I can assure you that, if you pursue this, within a year you'll have a baby." They left his office feeling elated. If they wanted to, it seemed, they would be able to adopt a white infant more or less from their own background.

Toward the end of October, the Jewish Family Service invited them to hear a lecture by Diane Michelsen. Lee was going to be away, but Dan saw the meeting as a chance to take some initiative. Michelsen's talk was about open adoption—a new direction for the Family Service. At the start of Paul Dubroff's years in the adoption field, eleven years before, he and his colleagues had prized confidentiality in adoption: in his view then, they helped adopting couples maintain the secrecy around their infertility, and they considered it a truism that birth mothers moved on with their lives after quietly placing a baby for adoption and that adoptees had no real need to know their biological roots. In part from his own experience (he has three children, two of them adopted), Dubroff felt that he had learned better. "I look back on that and I see that the world has changed," he said not long ago. "We now prepare people for an open process—meeting birth parents. We build that into our consultation, and we talk about the values of birth parents." From Diane Michelsen's point of view, Dubroff's approach was still relatively conservative, governed by a reluctant acceptance of open adoption as the wave of the future and by caution about the new and the unknown. (When couples adopting through the Family Service meet birth parents, for example, it is usually for one time only, without any exchange of identifying information like surnames or addresses.) But Michelsen also considered Dubroff a decent man, in charge of a good program, and was glad for the chance to spread the word to prospective adopters through his network.

At the meeting, Michelsen handed out a paper entitled "WHO ME? MEET THE BIRTHPARENTS? EEK!" It dealt with seven common reactions to open adoption from prospective adopters: fear of rejection ("What if she doesn't like me—because I'm too old/young, fat/skinny, liberal/conservative, rich/poor, have other children/don't have other children . . . or I say the wrong thing?"); envy ("I'm afraid it will be too difficult to meet with someone who's pregnant"); fear of "kidnapping" ("If she knows who I am or where I live, she will haunt my life forever"); fear of intrusion ("If I have contact with her . . . I will never be able to get her out of my life"); fear of facing another's pain and loss ("If I meet her, her pain will overshadow my joy"); fear of being a child thief ("I will feel like I'm stealing her child"); and vulnerability ("Are we inviting trouble to have direct contact?").

She went through the list of every person directly involved in an adoption (birth parents, adoptive parents, adoptee) and asked the people in the audience about the stereotypes that each role called to mind. She had brought with her some adoptive parents and a birth mother and asked them to speak, too. The birth mother made an impression on Dan: "The first couple she had interviewed as prospective parents she really liked a lot. She was nervous, a little bit angry that she had to give up this child, and a little bit angry that they could afford the baby. She got over that, and she liked them, and then they got pregnant and dumped her. She was incensed. Very vulnerable, an awful situation. She found another family and went with that family, but at that point was sort of angry and would ask, 'So how come you can't have kids? What's wrong with you?' Feeling powerless in her situation, she was striking out. I could see the potential for harm."

In December of 1987, the Stones began to make more inquiries about adoption. Paul Dubroff had given them a list of eleven lawyers and private agencies that might help them with a conventional adoption or an arrangement in which the lawyer or the agency introduced them to a birth mother and the Jewish Family Service handled the legal adoption. (Massachusetts is one of six states that prohibit private adoptions and require that independently arranged adoptions be channeled through state-licensed agencies.) The first office Lee and Dan called was that of a Vermont lawyer who said there was no room either in his adoption pool or on his waiting list. The second was that of a Vermont agency that specialized in teaching prospective adopters how to find their own birth mother. Dan: "That all sounded pretty grim to me. There was something about the advertising and the networking that seemed very oppressive. I had this image of handwritten notes up in Laundromats with pregnant women who were stoned on Tide."

At the start of 1988, before another round of fertility treatment, they decided to sign up with the Jewish Family Service, hoping to work with the Family Service and a lawyer. Unlike some conventional agencies, the Family Service didn't require prospective adopters to stop trying to conceive a baby. One of the steps in its procedure (as is the case with almost all agencies) was a home study for Dan and Lee, a state requirement now used as much to have prospective adopters focus on the distinctions of starting or expanding a family through adoption as to screen out those "unfit" to be adoptive parents. For a week in February, Lee became pregnant for the third time and began to worry that she would give birth to a "genetic disaster." She said, "I would go to the grocery store and I would come home and burst into tears." The day a social worker came to visit Dan and Lee as part of their home study, Lee was miscarrying. "Here I am going, 'Excuse me, I just have to go to the bathroom.' " Dan said, "We didn't know whether to tell the social worker. We didn't."

Another tenet of Rochelle Friedman's is that, even if a couple can conceive and give birth, there is no guarantee that they will produce the child they hope to. After the third miscarriage, Lee and Dan found this a comforting thought. They related it to a conviction that Diane Michelsen had expressed in her Jewish Family Service talk a few months before. Dan: "What Diane said is that by doing an open adoption you can have a relationship with the birth mother, and the birth mother with you, that helps deal with these feelings of being out of control." They could do for themselves what their genes might not, even if Lee carried a child of theirs to term, by choosing a birth mother with whom they felt a kinship. "Species recognition," Dan called this notion. "If you meet someone and you like them, there is something having to do with alikeness and humanness that puts you into an almost familial relationship. That idea relaxed us enormously."

The Family Service list of lawyers had included Michelsen, and Lee and Dan wrote her in the middle of March 1988. By return mail, she answered with more information about her practice. Dan's spring vacation was coming up, so, on the spur of the moment, he suggested that they call Michelsen to set up an appointment with her at her office in Walnut Creek, near San Francisco. The next week, they flew out West and spent a morning with Michelsen. The birth mother whom Dan had heard speak at the Jewish Family Service was now working as Michelsen's receptionist. The Stones and Michelsen hit it off. The lawyer described as "metaphysical" what would happen between them and a birth mother and said that, for people from the East Coast, the couple had a "high comfort level" about open adoption. The Stones explained that they weren't really Easterners. Lee grew up as a Denver debutante in what she called "an extremely conservative mainstream Wasp" family, and transformed herself at "a very progressive hippie" boarding school in Northern California before going to the University of California at Santa Cruz. She had come to Boston in the early seventies, and it had been her base since. Dan grew up in Santa Barbara. "Our house burned down in 1961 in one of those California fires, and my folks were divorced in 1964, one event leading to another in my mind," he said. He graduated from the University of California at Berkeley, worked adventurous jobs (forest ranger in Central America, group leader on scientific expeditions in Africa, boatman on whitewater river trips throughout the American West), and in the midseventies moved to Boston to go to graduate school at Harvard University.

The Stones and Michelsen concentrated on the résumé package, using two thick binders of other people's presentations as illustrations of what worked and what didn't. Lee and Dan had brought some favorite pictures of themselves. Michelsen found them too "clingy," "exclusive," and "camp." She wanted a picture that highlighted a beatific triangle—Lee, Dan, and room for the baby. Lee: "I kept saying *Diane*, this is just *media*, this is just *advertising*, we have to *sell* ourselves, we have to give this *incredible* picture—why else would a birth mother pick us? She told us she thought we'd go quickly, as a package, as a commodity."

Dan took a more knowing view of the package. He saw it as a combination of sincerity and artifice: "The idea is that you really want people to know who you are, so you attract like kinds. On the other hand, since you're dealing with a visual medium and since there's a limited amount of time for people to look at these books, all the contingencies that go into advertising are important. It's the combination of having something utterly crafted and artificial, and something quite authentic and personal and true. The two things together were fun to talk about. And also horrifying."

Michelsen told the Stones what had happened in the case of each of the people represented in the binders. A couple with a black standard poodle that was shown wearing red sunglasses were picked by a birth mother who loved dogs. A physically unattractive couple who were otherwise appealing were picked by a sexy birth mother who figured that others might not choose them and believed they would be great parents. Some went quickly, in a matter of weeks, but almost everyone who wanted to adopt was able to—within eleven months, on average. When the Stones left Michelsen, they were again elated. They drove to Berkeley, ate lunch, drove into the Berkeley Hills while going over their meeting, and ate another lunch.

Back East, it took six weeks for them to put their package together. When they finished, in the second week of May, Lee wanted to send the statement and pictures to Michelsen immediately. ("I'm the pessimist of the two. I said, 'We're never going to get a call. It's going to take a year and a half. Let's just do it.' ") Dan realized that once the material was in they were going to be in a position to have a child for the first time. He wanted to sit on the portfolio for a few days. He said, "The reality of that made me think I had to let go of the feeling of having our own biological child." They waited a week, and Lee mailed it. "The bun is in the oven," she recalls thinking.

Meeting

There weeks later, on Friday afternoon, June 10, Elizabeth Rice reached Lee at home. She said, "Hello, Lee. This is Elizabeth Rice, in Diane Michelsen's office. Good *news* for you. We have a birth mother." Lee froze. Rice continued, "Are you ready? Do you have a pencil? Here's some information about her: she's twenty years old, her name is Margaret Bass, she's got red hair, she describes herself as pear-shaped, she's a singer, she's majoring in marketing, she's an honor student, she's never been married, she's very much involved with her boyfriend, Tom, who is six feet three inches, has brown hair, and was in a stand-up comedy improv group. Margaret would like to call you. I just want to see if it would be O.K. if she called you."

Lee thanked Rice and asked if she could call back. Her first thought had been that a friend from her mind-body group was putting her on. When she decided that the call was real, she panicked. A few days before, she then remembered, she had been out with a pregnant friend and they had gone down a list of traits they hoped their babies wouldn't have. Both had said red hair. Lee called Dan at his office and said, "You are not going to believe this one! You are not going to believe it!

We got a call! We got a call! What are we going to do!? And she's got red hair!"

Dan confirmed the details with Rice, who warned that Peggy had promised to call Michelsen's office back and hadn't and that he and Lee should be prepared for the possibility that Peggy would never call again. Dan and Lee assumed they had twenty-four hours to consider her inquiry and let Rice know whether Peggy should call them. In the meantime, Peggy had called Rice back and Rice had given her the Stones' telephone number. Within two hours of her first contact with Michelsen's office, Peggy called Lee.

Lee: "Peggy has this very squeaky voice, and she sounded very sweet, and said, 'I'm so glad to have found you.' I said, 'What do you know about us?' " Peggy sketched the events that led to her call, including how Rice had read their résumé along with two others. Lee: "I said to myself, I bet it was because Dan's a botanist, because that's so exotic." Peggy told Lee that she needed to move away from home as soon as possible and that she was willing to come to Massachusetts. Lee replied, "It's wonderful talking to you, this is so exciting, but I'm so overwhelmed. I really want Dan to be here with me. Can you call at nine o'clock, collect?" Peggy said, "Sure. I get off work then."

In the next several hours, Dan and Lee pieced together a picture of the young woman and the young man who might be the birth mother and the birth father of their child. "The lawyer had said we had good senses of humor," Dan recalled. "And Peggy had said, 'Oh, great, my boyfriend's a stand-up comic,' and for the rest of the afternoon I kept thinking that that was odd, but that there was something terrific about it. These qualities welled up, surfaced out of the essential protoplasm of eggs and sperms out there. Ours didn't seem to work together, for whatever reason, but out of all those other eggs and sperms, a few qualities emerged: honor student; singer; stand-up comic."

Dan also found himself thinking about the nature of adoption in a way he hadn't before. He realized that he thought adoption could be painful for adoptees, that adopted children sometimes asked, Why me? His own view of adoptees from when he was a boy, he decided, was patronizing. That upset him: "I had some feeling like, Too bad, it's not as good as I have it, I have my own mother whom I love and who loves me and it's really wonderful and this person doesn't love you as much, probably, and it must be a little cold in there."

By nine o'clock, he had worked himself into a state of intense ambivalence. Peggy did not call at nine, and that made it worse. At 9:15, Lee declared that they had suffered another stroke of bad luck. At 9:20, the phone rang. Dan picked up, and it was Peggy. She said, "The baby's been kicking wildly since I talked to your wife!" She called him Mr. Stone. "You can't call me Mr. Stone," he protested. "You're the mother of my child!" They both liked that, and Dan thought, he said later, This is good, this is fine, this is wonderful. Peggy told them that she had been an au-pair girl and that she was now working in a toy store. Lee kept slipping Dan questions to ask Peggy: "How are you feeling? What was it like finding out you were pregnant? Did you think you wanted to keep it? Describe your background: parents, sisters, brothers. What would happen if your parents found out?" She whispered to Dan, "Have her send us a picture so it won't be a shock when we meet!" She handed him more questions: "What will you do after the baby? Describe your interests." She repeated, "What will you do after the baby?"

Peggy answered all the questions. She had spent a lot of time with the parents of newborns, she said. Those were special times, and she didn't want to interfere with the Stones'. After the baby, she went on, she would get back to Wilmington as soon as possible. And she wanted to find out about Lee and Dan. Did they really want the baby, or did it just "fit into their schedule"? Were they happy together, or did they hope a baby would "save their marriage"? If the baby turned out to have something wrong with it, would they still adopt it? ("If you want a baby, you want a baby," Peggy observed later. "You don't pick and choose.")

Peggy also told Dan how much she loved Tom. Dan asked her what it would be like to give up the baby and still be with him. Peggy said she didn't believe the child was meant for them; it was like a package delivered to the wrong address. "I don't want to sound too goody two-shoes, but we think just well enough of ourselves to believe what we're doing is pretty great," Peggy said. To her, giving up the baby for adoption was like donating a kidney to another person. She said, "A part of my life is going to be a permanent part of yours." Peggy also said she was willing to go on welfare in order to keep her living expenses down during the last two months of pregnancy and qualify for state payment of her hospital bills.

The conversation lasted about half an hour. It was fluid, light, intense, and pleasing to all of them. By the end of it, Peggy felt that she had really connected with Dan, and Dan was confident that he could go through with an adoption. He suggested that they all meet soon.

The following Wednesday, Lee and Dan got a letter from Peggy. Enclosed was a sonogram image of the fetus, taken at twenty-seven weeks and four days. "Dear Dan and Lee," the letter began, "I'm dashing this off right after having talked to you. I am so happy to have found you all. This is so perfect it is obviously meant to be, this child will have the most wonderful parents in the whole world, and I got to match you all up." The letter reported that the baby was physically very active, and said, "You all are so lucky that you aren't doing the hatching of this one, Lee would be black and blue." It also said, "Your baby has been kicking non-stop, it literally shook change from my pants pocket."

The letter gave some background on Peggy and Tom: Tom was Thomas C. Spaeth, Jr. ("C is for Carter, yes like the President"); everyone in Peggy's family had Morris for a middle name ("I don't know why"); they both loved "children, animals, doll houses, toys, kaleidoscopes, cooking (me), eating (him), 'Far Side' comics, music (him), operettas (me), Redskins (us), purple, high-tech equipment (him)." Peggy wrote, "I think I'm very funny, but I let Tom take all the credit." As a postscript, she added, "By the way, I hope you all are dark-haired because I ain't birthin' no blonde." Lee and Dan were completely taken with the letter. It did for Lee what the phone conversation with Peggy had done for Dan. "When I got to 'Your baby . . . ,' " Lee said, "I lost it."

Saturday, June 18, the Stones flew to Washington, D.C., to meet Peggy and Tom, who got there by train. They had arranged a rendezvous at National Airport at one o'clock. Dan and Lee arrived early. As they tried to pick Peggy and Tom out of the crowd, Dan took some pictures of a wall clock: 12:55; 1:12; 1:19. Around one-thirty, Peggy and Tom arrived, holding hands.

Peggy is of medium height. Beneath her red curly hair, she has a round, freckly face. Her chin is pronounced and the crest of her upper lip (she calls it her beak) juts out slightly. She wore black stretch pants, a turquoise smock with black stripes, a white baseball jacket, and a baseball cap. Her glasses, which were oversized, rested near the tip of her nose. Tom is a head taller than Peggy. He has dark, wide-set eyes that give him a brooding look, and mild acne covered by a close-cropped beard. He was wearing blue jeans and an open-neck shirt and, like Peggy, black Chinese slippers. Both looked very young.

Lee has a patrician face with a fine nose and jaw, and alert blue eyes. She is about Peggy's height, has a long, quick stride, and is slim and beautiful. She wore a collarless print dress, in a pattern of pink, blue, and green. Dan is three inches taller than Lee. He has an oblong face, a long nose, and a thick, trim beard, and his brown hair is cut short on top. When he smiles, his face mobilizes. Otherwise, he has a bemused, sober look. Like Tom, he wore jeans and an open-neck shirt. He happened not to be wearing Chinese slippers, though he and Lee often did at home.

Peggy felt the baby kick as soon as she noticed Lee and Dan, she said. They sized up how Peggy and Tom were dressed, and thought: *Total* species recognition. Lee walked up to Peggy and, hugging her, said, "I'm a blonde!" Peggy reacted shyly. On the phone and in her letter, she had seemed fresh and ebullient. In person, Dan found her cool and official. Lee and Dan felt like the youngsters meeting the established couple. Peggy and Tom hadn't known how old Dan and Lee were. While they looked about the age they had put on their résumé (late thirties, or old enough to have had three miscarriages and "to be able to afford an adoption"), they also seemed tired and strung out. The first thing they all talked about was whether the others had eaten. Lee said she was starved; Peggy handed her some grapes, and she polished off the bunch.

On the subway into Washington, the men stood and the women sat. They all talked about a recent exhibition of Georgia O'Keeffe's paintings at the National Gallery of Art, and in part because each exchange seemed potentially so revealing, the conversation felt like work. Peggy mentioned that her father knew Randy Newman, a songwriter whom Lee and Dan like, and Lee kicked Dan. ("Randy Newman! Kaboom!" Dan said later.) They went to the Old Post Office–Pavilion on Pennsylvania Avenue, and split up to buy different kinds of fast food. (Peggy and Dan chose Indian, Lee got Mexican, and Tom ordered a hamburger.) When they joined up again, they weren't sure what to do: there were no tables available on the plaza outside, where they had hoped to eat; it was windy and felt chilly; and neither couple knew whether the other would be comfortable sitting on the ground. They ended up nearby on a stone curb surrounding the arcade of the Internal Revenue Service Building, not far from where a steel band played.

Peggy started up the conversation. She said she wanted to ask a lot of "June Cleavery questions" (what kind of a home the Stones lived in, whether they had a yard), but Lee and Dan didn't hear many questions. According to them, Peggy delivered a monologue about her pregnancy and some of her views of child-rearing (she hoped they wouldn't push the baby too fast and that Lee wouldn't work full-time), and didn't ask them about themselves. It occurred to Dan that he hadn't planned well for the meeting and that, beyond learning some basics (he asked whether Peggy's and Tom's families had histories of any striking genetically inherited traits or illnesses, and was educated about baldness on both sides), he didn't know what he wanted to tell them. Lee and Dan considered the meeting a chance for all of them to decide whether they wanted to go ahead with an adoption: the reason for pursuing it openly was to feel that they had a choice. Peggy and Tom seemed to have made up their minds. Peggy repeated that she needed to leave Wilmington and said she could be ready to go within days. Lee was struck by how elegantly Peggy sat in a lotus-like position. Seeing how well she carried herself and how hard it was to tell that she was pregnant, Lee and Dan let go of their doubts that her family didn't know.

Tom said little for most of the time they were together. Toward the end, he made a short speech. He said that he and Peggy didn't expect to be involved with the Stones after the adoption; they didn't want to know a lot about the child, although they were willing to keep in touch if Lee and Dan wished to. But they had one request: if the child died, they wanted to know about it. They didn't want to imagine the child living if it was gone. He and Peggy had already written letters to the baby, Tom said, and they wanted to pass the letters on through Lee and Dan. Tom said he had a final question. Did Lee and Dan love each other? ("I tend to put paper and flowers over everything," Peggy said later. "Tom tends to scrape paper and flowers off.") Dan said that Tom's was a good question, and that they did, very much.

Peggy and Tom liked the Stones a lot, and Peggy decided to send them a subscription to the magazine *American Baby*. Peggy thought she had seen in Lee's eyes the "hungry look" that "needs to be there when you want to be a mom." Tom felt he could trust them to take care of Peggy when she was away from him. Lee and Dan concluded that Peggy and Tom were "extraordinary." Lee said, "We were very happy." The conversation had lasted most of the afternoon.

On Monday, Peggy told her parents that she had got an offer to work in Boston for the summer, dividing her time between baby-sitting and doing telemarketing for a real-estate database firm. The job she described was similar to one that a classmate had actually taken. Peggy had been on a jet only once before, when she went with Tom's family to Disney World, in Florida, the previous October; she billed the Boston experience as a chance to travel before settling down to full-time work after graduation the following year. Her parents gave their approval. To make the job seem real to them, Peggy pretended to speak by phone with a professor of hers who she said had arranged the job. On the other end of the line, Tom played the part of the professor. Peggy left for Boston two days later.

History

From the days of the "orphan trains" which, between 1854 and 1929, delivered over a hundred thousand waifs, "street arabs," and juvenile delinquents from New York City to families in towns out West, adoption has been said to embody a distinctly American ideal. In England, adoption was not permitted by statute until this century, because social status and, thus, identity were seen as being determined by bloodline alone. The United States was a nation of immigrants who adjusted to new surroundings, made fresh starts, and shaped their own destinies, like children who were adopted.

The history of adoption in America has in fact been framed less by an ideal than by a series of social compacts. The "orphan trains" (misleadingly named, since perhaps three-fourths of the children on the trains had living parents who had abandoned them) were invented by Charles Loring Brace, a Protestant minister who believed that the Lower East Side's "society of irreclaimable little vagabonds" could only be saved in "God's Reformatory"—good homes which taught the gospels of work, education, religion, and self-reliance and which were located in "pure country." The trains were sponsored by the Children's Aid Society, which Brace helped found and which considered its relocation program a remarkable success. A picture of a properly dressed, unsmiling blond girl in a 1910 report on the "Emigration or Placing Out System" is captioned: "A little waif taken from an institution and placed in a home in the West, and adopted. She has just made a European tour with her foster parents."

The families that took in such children often lived on farms and valued extra hands. Unlike earlier arrangements between orphan asylums and foster families in this country, which were modeled on the kind of servitude allowed by England's poor laws and bound children by contract to give their labor in exchange for room and board, the Children's Aid Society placements weren't formal indenture. One of Brace's innovations was that the arrangements were for free, no strings attached. In theory, if either the family or the child was unhappy, they could end the relationship and the agency would find the child another home.

But families seeking children from the orphan trains chose them, in effect, through a form of auction: children wore name tags and performed short acts for potential foster parents and then lined up to be picked at a local church or courthouse. Siblings sometimes stayed together but often didn't. While the Children's Aid Society kept a list of the "creditable members of society" who once rode the trains (including a couple of governors, of North Dakota and the Alaska Territory), the agency's methods were discredited by some, in part because the agency opposed formal adoption: few of the children it placed were legally adopted. When a researcher named Evelyn Sheets interviewed some of the aging survivors of the trains in the mid-1980s, she gathered memories of sadness, deprivation, and abuse that counterbalanced the Society's stories of pampering and welcome.

The Society's opposition to formal adoption was then the rule for all orphanages. Around the turn of the century, few legal adoptions actually took place, compared with the number of children in institutional or informal care, because many people felt ambivalent about adoption. Believing in the teachings of eugenics, which held that poor, immigrant, and unwed mothers were "feebleminded" and likely to give birth to children of similarly low capacity, many doubted that the children available for adoption could be saved. Child-welfare experts cultivated this prejudice by opposing the placement of infants until their character and capabilities were proved.

Until the end of the nineteenth century, couples in many states could adopt only by having a "special bill" passed in the state legislature or by registering a child as chattel, like a plow or a bull. (Limited laws allowing adoption were passed in 1846 by Mississippi and in 1850 by Texas and Vermont; they required the filing of a deed with a county court.) The callousness of those laws was preferable to that of unlicensed maternity homes and other facilities that, in exchange for money, promised pregnant women they would "adopt out" the women's babies and sometimes did so, as one historian put it, by arranging "to have the child starved, drugged, or suffocated to death."

By 1929, every state had an adoption law. European countries had based their rules on Roman law, whose main purpose was to assure the orderly transfer of property through inheritance: the French Civil Code of 1902 required an adopter to be at least fifty years old and to have no heirs, and an adoptee to be old enough to inherit. In the United States, on the other hand, most state laws followed the Massachusetts model, the first comprehensive state law on adoption, which was passed in 1851 and required that adopters be "of sufficient ability to bring up the child, and furnish suitable nurture and education": the laws required that an adoption be approved by a judge, and sought to provide an adopted child with a permanent home pledged to safeguarding his best interests.

Since the turn of the century, there has been a running debate in the adoption world about how best to accomplish those ends. During the fifty preceding years, the best-interests standard was defined primarily in terms of economics. After

1900, the discussion broadened to include a child's psychological well-being. In 1909, President Theodore Roosevelt hosted a White House Conference on Children and Youth, which concluded that poverty alone should not be grounds for removing children from families; where possible, they should remain with their biological parents. The Conference endorsed the maxim that "home life" was the "highest and finest product of civilization, the great molding force of mind and character." The next best alternative was a "carefully selected" foster or adoptive home. To oversee the matching of children with homes, the Conference recommended the establishment of a voluntary organization of agencies to help children. In 1920, the Child Welfare League of America emerged in that role.

The perfection of infant formula as a substitute for breast milk in the late 1920s led to the modern era of adoption: for the first time, even couples who could not afford a wet nurse could adopt and nurture a baby soon after birth. As that idea took hold, it was reflected in a growing preference for younger versus older children. The Children's Bureau of the United States government found, in a Depression-era study of adoption in ten major states, that fifty-nine percent of the adoptees were born out of wedlock; as high as forty-one percent were born of married couples who could not afford, or weren't prepared, to raise them.

In 1938, the Child Welfare League of America approved ten minimum safeguards for adoption: on behalf of the child, among other things, it recommended that "the family asking for him have a good home and good family life to offer" and that he be "wanted for the purpose of completing an otherwise incomplete family group"; for the adopting family, that "the child have the intelligence and the physical and mental background to meet [their] reasonable expectations" and that the "adoption proceedings be completed without unnecessary publicity"; and, for the state, that "there be a trial period of residence of reasonable length for the best interests of the family and the child" and that "the adoption procedure be sufficiently flexible to avoid encouragement of illegitimacy on the one hand and trafficking in babies on the other." The League proposed no safeguards on behalf of the birth parents.

The League's standards reflected principles of modern adoption more recently identified by Joan Hollinger, a professor at the University of Detroit School of Law: that the adoptive family fully replace the biological one; that the adoption be permanent; that the adoption take place as early as possible after the child's birth, to increase its chances of success; and that the adoption be confidential. In retrospect, a Minnesota law passed in 1917 which included the first American provision about confidentiality focused on a key element of modern adoption. In the nineteen-thirties and forties, there was a concerted effort across the country to pass laws that sealed the legal records of adoptions. (Some statutes sealed the records of adoption hearings but left open the records of adoption agencies or permitted everyone, including adult adoptees, to inspect the state's original birth certificates.)

Confidentiality was said to serve three main purposes: protecting adoptees from the stigma of being born out of wedlock, for the original birth certificates of adoptees disclosed their legal status, often labeling an adoptee "Bastard" or "Illegitimate"; granting birth parents anonymity, by hiding their part in a birth out of wedlock; and giving adoptive families the opportunity to develop like biological ones, in part by protecting them from birth parents who might otherwise seek out the child they had produced.

"Reporters, nosing around for news, might come upon something really juicy and publish it, causing untold suffering and permanent damage," C. S. Prentiss wrote in 1940. "Unscrupulous relatives could trace a child if they wished and use their knowledge to upset a well-established relationship, if they did not do worse, and use it for actual blackmail."

Confidentiality laws protected adoptees and birth parents from the shame of illegitimacy, and adoptive parents from the shame of infertility. In effect, they enforced a bargain of silence which most states backed to serve their own interest in finding permanent homes for children. A nineteen-forties textbook on adoption stated: "Most of the children so born are a source of embarrassment to everybody concerned, and both the mother and the child usually need help if they are to have any chance of winning back into ordinary social life." The deal was strengthened by a view about the psychology of adoption that prevailed until this generation: it was in the best interests of the adopted child for adoptive parents to treat them as if they were not adopted, and for adoptees not to know their birth parents. Adoption was "perhaps the most permanent relationship" that society could create, one scholar observed, and its chances of success were boosted by treating it like a work of nature.

During the Second World War, the increase in the number of brief, intimate relationships between men and women led to a substantial increase in the number of adoptions (in 1944, the number of adoption petitions in the United States was three times what it had been ten years before). The illicit nature of those affairs strengthened the appeal of confidentiality. By the nineteen-fifties, all the states had approved sealed-record provisions, and the number of "unrelated" adoptions (adults adopting children not related by blood, in the best-known kind of adoption) continued to grow steadily: from 33,800 in 1951, according to a respected estimate, to a peak of 89,200 in 1970, before slipping back to a plateau of approximately 50,000 a year for the past decade and a half.

The year 1970 was a watershed for a number of reasons. Adoption was affected by some basic shifts in social patterns that had become significant in the half decade before. Men and women had begun to marry later, have fewer children, divorce far more often, and leave behind roles they assumed after the Second World War. The increase in households headed by divorced single women diminished the stigma against single parents in general, and some young women who previously would have felt obliged to give up their babies for adoption decided to keep them. The feminist movement reinforced such acts of self-sufficiency, and while the rate of out-of-wedlock births doubled, the percentage of single mothers who gave up their babies dropped sharply. Birth control had recently been sanctioned by the United States Supreme Court and, widely practiced with the advent of the pill, led to fewer births than otherwise might have occurred. Abortion was already legal in a few states (in 1973, in the landmark case of *Roe* v. *Wade*, the Supreme Court legalized it nationwide), so that some babies who otherwise might have been given up for adoption were not born.

A transformation in thinking about how adoption might serve the best interests of the child followed. It can be seen simply as a function of supply and demand. In the nineteen-twenties, adopting couples sometimes picked their babies from rows of newborn infants at large maternity homes. By the thirties, adoption agencies substituted their own judgments about which couple should be matched with which baby; in 1934, the Children's Bureau questioned whether adoption agencies were "too selective in the children" whom they were "accepting for placement," but there were still more available babies than interested adopters, by most estimates.

In 1955, at a national conference on adoption, Irene Josselyn, a Chicago psychiatrist, criticized the practice of using an adopted child "as a means to give a bored woman something to do, as a new toy with which adults could play, as a cure for the neurosis of a childless woman, as a way to meet the lacks in a woman's marriage because her husband was too busy with business or too interested in alcohol to be interested in her, or as a tool for preserving a disintegrating marriage." Another participant, H. L. Shapiro, the curator of physical anthropology at the American Museum of Natural History in New York City, remarked on "the growing conviction that the welfare and development of the child is the primary concern of agencies responsible for their placement and not simply satisfying the desire of a couple for a child or the mere transference of a child from institutional to familial care."

Still, through the nineteen-sixties, the best-interests standard was often satisfied by what served the interests of adopting couples. In California, for example, the supply-demand equation continued to favor couples, and those who wanted to adopt four or more children had no trouble doing so. Handicapped, minority, and older children (aged seven or more) were considered "hard to place" and sometimes were judged "unadoptable." So were mixed-race children.

In the late sixties, however, as couples with biological children began adopting third and fourth children for humanitarian reasons (they thought it was wrong to have more than two biological children but wanted to have larger families; they felt a moral impetus to welcome into their families children who otherwise wouldn't have one), the range—in age and background—of children who were adopted also expanded. "Hard to place" became "special needs."

Not long after, the number of infertile couples began to increase. According to the National Center for Health Statistics, the rate of infertility held relatively constant beginning in 1965, but the number of infertile couples grew as the baby boom, the largest American generation of potential parents, matured and delayed childbearing. Other experts contended that the rate itself increased. To them, couples were waiting until their thirties to try to conceive children and discovered that the risks of miscarriage for women over thirty-five were much higher than for women in their twenties. Women whose mothers had taken a synthetic estrogen called DES (diethylstilbestrol) to keep from miscarrying, from 1945 until it was taken off the market, in 1971, often had abnormalities of the vagina and cervix, and more difficulty than other women in carrying a fetus to term. Use of alcohol and drugs, exposure to pesticides, and other factors also increased the rate of infertility in men and women, some experts claimed. By some accounts, the fraction of infertile couples rose from about one in ten in the nineteen-fifties to about one in six in the mid-seventies. To the National Center for Health Statistics, the factors that might have led to an increase in the rate of infertility were counterbalanced by improvements in fertility treatment and in its use, and the rate in the midseventies remained at about one in ten.

By then, the number of couples waiting to adopt had become significantly larger than the number of healthy infants available for adoption. By one controversial estimate, the ratio reached forty to one. Some experts said that figure was greatly exaggerated. A paper issued by the National Institute of Child and Human Development, the first based on analysis of data from interviews, found that the ratio was three to one in 1988, when demographic and other factors affecting the ratio were not dramatically different from those in the midseventies.

Some major changes in views about the psychology of adoption occurred about the same time as the shift in the relationship between supply and demand, and undoubtedly received more attention as a result of it. In 1964, H. David Kirk's book *Shared Fate* argued that, contrary to the prevailing theory, adoptive families were different—and had to be—from biological families. When adoptive families acted as if they were identical with biological ones and ignored their differences, the children were more apt to have difficulties in development and the parents to encounter problems in their own roles. When adoptive families acknowledged the differences between themselves and biological families—that the parents and children shared a mutual need—the parents were more likely to empathize with the feelings of the birth parents who had placed children for adoption, successfully to guide the adoptees in resolving questions they might have about their identities, and to create and nurture the adoptees' connection to their adoptive families.

The critical side of Kirk's views seemed to be borne out by

an eruption of protest about past adoption practices. Organizations were founded by adoptees searching for their biological roots. In 1953, Jean Paton had started the Life History Study Center, in Philadelphia, to gather reports from adoptees and "to give emphasis to the view that adoption—among other human institutions—is a process which influences individual life for many years beyond its initiation." One of Paton's missions was to encourage and help adoptees search for their roots, through an organization that grew out of the Study Center— Orphan Voyage. She is sometimes called the mother of the adoption-reform movement.

It took a generation for her point of view to gain wide support. The Adoptees' Liberty Movement Association, now the largest search group, was organized in 1971. Its manifesto declares, among other things, that "it is an affront to human dignity and civil rights to be denied access to one's birth records" and that "adoptees are victims of an 'adoption game' in which they are forced to believe their birthparents are insignificant or dead and that their adoptive parents are their real parents." Groups representing the other parties to adoption, the birth parents (for example, Concerned United Birthparents) and the adoptive parents (Adoptive Parents for Open Records), issued their own charges. The adoption postulates widely accepted since they were first issued, in 1938, by the Child Welfare League were subjected to increasingly agitated criticism.

Controversy in the adoption world was not new. Soon after the Second World War, for example, white couples began adopting black children, and the trend ebbed and flowed in modest numbers for the next two decades. Initially, the practice called into question a basic tenet of adoption. In the nineteen-fifties, agencies commonly tried to match children and adoptive parents by intellectual potential, religion, temperament, education, physical resemblance, cultural and national backgrounds, and other factors, especially race. In 1972, the National Association of Black Social Workers made transracial adoption a political matter, by taking what it called "a vehement stand against the placement of black children in white homes for any reason." Black leaders described the practice as "cultural genocide," arguing that whites were obliterating the racial identity of blacks. By their strong opposition, they all but stopped it for several years.

On the other hand, in a widely discussed series of studies conducted in the nineteen-seventies, Rita James Simon and Howard Alstein concluded that transracial adoption offered the promise of a revolution in racial attitudes, leading to true color-blindness: blacks adopted by whites saw themselves as black, the researchers found, but had positive attitudes about their white families and whites in general; they were indifferent to the advantages of being white in America, and comfortable with the racial identity that their appearance gave them. The Simon–Alstein findings were corroborated to some degree by other work.

Yet, for all its intensity, the debate about transracial adoption was eclipsed by the debate about whether it was proper for adoptees to seek detailed knowledge of their genetic background and, in some cases, contact with their biological parents. Adoptees embarked on this project ("Have you searched?" is what some adoptees ask each other) to understand themselves better, to get medical information, for a sense of connection, to fill an emptiness, and to ask why their birth parents gave them up. Some claimed that the sealed records making unofficial searches necessary violated the U.S. Constitution by denying adoptees equal protection of the law. They cited as a precedent for changes in American law the longtime practice in Scotland of maintaining open records, which, since 1975, has been followed throughout Great Britain. One researcher estimated that forty percent of American adoptees wished to learn the names of or to meet their birth parents.

Opponents of open records claimed that only a small percentage of adoptees in Great Britain had actually searched (0.3

percent of adopted adults in England and Wales and 0.7 percent in Scotland, between 1980 and 1982, which extrapolates to perhaps one-fifth of all British adoptees over a lifetime, if each year during the fifty years of adulthood a different small percentage of adoptees search), and that only two percent of American adoptees have searched. As a compromise, the opponents proposed voluntary-consent adoption registries (now used in twenty-two states) through which birth parents and adoptees named on the original birth certificate could communicate their willingness to meet but, until they did so, would be protected against the state's release of identifying information. Anything less controlled, the argument went, jeopardized the confidentiality promised to all parties in past adoptions and made it likely that more potential adoptions would end in abortion.

Supporters of the right to search contended that the mutual-consent registries were poorly advertised, complicated to use, and made a reunion between an adoptee and a birth parent a matter of luck; they pointed out that states could protect the confidentiality of past adoptions and still open records for the future. Some also acknowledged the problems searchers might face once they found their birth parents (adoptees being rejected by birth parents; adoptees and birth parents disappointing each other), and the need for adoptees, in particular, to have good counseling while they searched or even as they were deciding whether to search.

The most reform-minded admitted that their goal was to put an end to all confidentiality in adoption. The search movement expanded into something much bigger as the central disagreement in the adoption world began to focus on the relationships between adoptees and birth parents, and between birth and adoptive parents. It took on the stature of a philosophical conflict, for, among those concerned, the two most prevalent answers to the question, Should adoptions be confidential or open? reflected points of view that seemed irreconcilable.

The Open Movement

The concept of open adoption was initially proposed in 1976 in an article by Annette Baran and Reuben Pannor, two California social workers, and Arthur Sorosky, a psychiatrist. Their thesis was that, in the previous several years, the needs that adoption was intended to satisfy had evolved dramatically but theory hadn't. The new developments that moved them to offer their expert reappraisal were the increase in the number of challenges by adult adoptees to the practice of sealing birth records, and the increase in the number of unwed mothers who had chosen to raise their children instead of placing them for adoption.

Baran, Pannor, and Sorosky defined an open adoption as "one in which the birth parents meet the adoptive parents, participate in the separation and placement process, relinquish all legal, moral and nurturing rights to the child, but retain the right to continuing contact and to knowledge of the child's whereabouts and welfare." The impetus for the concept was practical. They had discovered that some young single mothers who in the past would have placed their children for adoption were running into serious problems raising them. Many of their children were ending up in and out of foster homes, and suffering. "The young single mothers who have an emotional attachment—whether positive or negative—to their children desperately need a new kind of adoption placement in which they can actively participate," the three wrote. "They want the security of knowing they have helped provide their children with a loving, secure existence and yet have not denied themselves the possibility of knowing them in the future."

To the authors, everyone who was a party to an open adoption seemed to benefit. A child who otherwise would have been "deprived" could have "a permanent home and reliable parental care." He would be less likely to feel rejected by his birth mother if he had some contact with her, and more likely to understand what led to his adoption. The birth mother was more likely to move on to a satisfying life and to be able to handle any feelings of guilt and loss derived from giving up the child. The adoptive parents were more likely to have an honest relationship with their child and to deal better with any fears they had about the birth mother coming to reclaim the child.

The authors had a hard time getting their article published. When it finally appeared in the journal *Social Work* (it was later included as a chapter in their book *The Adoption Triangle*), it ended on a discordant note that told something about the strength of the resistance they had encountered. On the one hand, the piece was chiding. ("What is currently lacking in the profession," Baran and Pannor stated about their fellow social workers, with the psychiatrist Sorosky's concurrence, "is the willingness to consider adoption that allows the birth mother a continuing role in her child's life.") On the other, it was measured: "Open adoption is not a panacea and should not be considered a suitable procedure for all birth or adoptive parents. It is, however, a viable approach in specific situations and can offer an acceptable solution to an otherwise insoluble problem."

Without orchestration, a small number of adoption agencies around the country had already begun to respond to needs like the one observed by Baran, Pannor, and Sorosky, and had moved toward open adoption. In 1974, two teenage birth parents working with the Children's Home Society of California, the state's largest agency, asked to meet the adoptive parents before the baby's placement, and the agency obliged. ("We didn't publicize the meeting because we weren't sure we should have done it," a former executive of the agency said.) In 1977, the same thing happened at the Child Saving Institute in Omaha, Nebraska. That year, as well, the San Antonio office of the Lutheran Social Service of Texas began to let birth and adoptive parents exchange letters and pictures, and by 1981 that office and another of the agency in Corpus Christi were arranging meetings between parents. Catholic Social Services of Green Bay, Wisconsin, thoroughly revised its approach. On the assumption that adoptees had the right to know everything about their heritage, it began to require birth parents to supply detailed autobiographies and it requested pictures of them and their families. A handful of new agencies were founded expressly to promote contact between birth and adoptive families.

The independence of these stirrings resulted in different definitions of openness in adoption by various agencies. Diane Yost, the program director for foster-care adoption at the Children's Home and Aid Society of Illinois, observed, "Openness can mean openness to hearing history about the biological family all the way through to completely open arrangements in which both families meet and have access to one another in some way throughout the years." A 1983 book titled *Dear Birthmother* by Phylis Speedlin and Kathleen Silber, the former director of the San Antonio office of the Lutheran Social Service of Texas, contains correspondence between adoptive and birth parents that offers a refutation of adoption "myths" (e.g., "the birthmother obviously doesn't care about her child or she wouldn't have given him away") and indicates the advantages of open adoption. The book is sometimes used by agencies as an easygoing introduction to the concept, and defines it broadly as any adoption that permits some form of communication between birth and adoptive parents. A group of adoption professionals called the Ad Hoc Committee to Reevaluate Adoptive Placement Philosophy took the same inclusive line. They described open adoption, however practiced, as an affirmation that "an adoptee, although relinquished and a full member of his/her adoptive family, nevertheless remains connected to his/her birth family."

The Ad Hoc Committee held the first national conference on open adoption in 1982. Two of the participants were Annette Baran and Reuben Pannor. In the half-dozen years since their initial article was published, their views had taken on a polemical consistency. "The secrecy, anonymity, and mystique surrounding the traditional adoptions of the past have left behind numerous psychological problems for adoptees, birth parents, and adoptive parents," they declared in a 1984 article called "Open Adoption as Standard Practice," adapted from a presentation that Pannor made at the conference. "This practice should not be perpetuated but must be replaced by a form of adoption that practices openness and honesty, and thereby permits a healthier and psychologically sounder adoption practice." They concluded unequivocally: "All adoptions should fall within the open adoption framework."

By the mid-eighties, however, the views of the Baran–Pannor team no longer marked the outer boundary of American thinking about adoption. A book titled *Cooperative Adoption*, by Mary Jo Rillera and Sharon Kaplan, a California adoption counselor, and, like *Dear Birthmother* and other books that are popular in the adoption world, published by a small press, identified the frontier. The book has a soft, New Age aura (an early chapter begins, "One of the most valuable tools for preparing to expand relationships and family is to view yourself and all other participants as whole"), and its guiding premise is a firm declaration of adoptees' rights.

"Cooperative adoption is knowing that children all come into this life whole, with all rights and relationships intact,"

Rillera and Kaplan state. "And it is understanding that no one has the right to interrupt those rights or deprive another being of them." By separating an adopted child from his birth family and his biological roots, confidential adoption, in their view, cuts him off from parts of his identity, jeopardizes his sense of continuity, and limits his opportunity to feel connected. It takes away his "right to self-determination." Cooperative adoption—in which adoptive and birth parents maintain an open relationship regarding the child—restores that right. For the authors, almost every detail about a cooperative adoption is negotiable: what the parents call each other (popular terms in cooperative adoptions are "bioparent" and "psychoparent," for psychological parent); what each pledges to do for the child (e.g., "be honest, never withhold information, provide financial support"); whether they will sustain a relationship after the adoption takes place, or bow out of each other's lives. But, in the authors' view, cooperative adoption "adds options and extends family relationships," as opposed to cutting off essential ties.

It is virtually undisputed that the movement for openness in adoption took hold outside, and in spite of, adoption agencies. It was led by the rank and file, birth and adoptive parents, with the established institutions following rather than leading in the transition. Some agencies have given up their long-standing commitment to confidential adoptions in part to win back the interest of birth and adoptive parents and to maintain their role as a mediator between them.

A map depicting where the practice of open adoption has taken hold in the United States during the past fifteen years would have two basic symbols. In bold letters would be clusters of capital A's, representing the growing number of adoptions carried out through agencies that deliberately endorse and offer some version of open adoption. In light letters would be groups of capital I's, standing for adoptions that are also open to some degree, arranged independently of agencies. The bold letters for agency adoptions and light letters for independent adoptions reflect the uncertainty of estimates about the number of independent adoptions. There are no uniform statistics about adoptions in the United States; although Congress has mandated that the Executive Branch begin collecting such data again by 1991, the federal government only gathered comprehensive figures between 1957 and 1975. The National Committee For Adoption, a lobbying organization for conventional agencies, estimates that one-third of the adoptions of unrelated children in the United States are independent adoptions. Some experts say that the fraction is half, and one claims that the figure is closer to four out of five.

Independent adoptions remain difficult to assess because, except in the states where they are illegal, they are, by and large, minimally regulated. They can happen much faster than agency adoptions and can have happy endings. They tend to cost more than agency adoptions; "baby-selling"—the sale of babies illegally for very high sums ($5,000 in the nineteen-forties, $50,000 today)—has recurred in cycles in this country since the late nineteenth century, and occurs almost exclusively through independent arrangements. They also have a greater chance of falling through or breaking down, with no money-back guarantee: it is possible for a couple to spend $20,000 and not end up with a child. Independent arrangements tend to be associated with the darkest adoption stories: Michele Launders paid Joel Steinberg, a Manhattan lawyer, five hundred dollars to arrange an independent adoption for her daughter, Elizabeth; it never took place, because Steinberg and his longtime companion, Hedda Nussbaum, kept—and abused—the little girl without formally adopting her.

In 1988, half a century after it published a list of its initial safeguards, the Child Welfare League of America dramatically revised its standards for adoption. Indirectly, the League took a position about the question of transracial adoption. "Children in need of adoption have a right to be placed into a family that reflects their ethnic or cultural heritage," it declared. "Children should not have their adoption denied or significantly delayed, however, when adoptive parents of other ethnic or cultural groups are available." It also declared itself opposed to independent adoptions. On behalf of its constituency of social workers, the League advised: "Regulation and control of adoptive placements, accompanied by expansion and improvement of services, are required in order to assure maximum protection for the child, birth parents, and adoptive parents." As to open adoption, the League avoided the leading edge of reform notions such as cooperative adoption; it defined the rights of children primarily in terms of care and protection rather than self-determination. But, in a major break from its former stand, the League asserted: "Adopted individuals, birth families, and adoptive families are best served by a process that is open and honest; one that supports the concept that all information, including identifying information, may be shared between birth and adoptive families." The concept of openness should be "an integral part of all adoption services," the League went on, with the "degree of openness" arrived at "by mutual agreement" among everyone involved.

The Adoption Fairy

Peggy had guessed that Boston would be colder than Wilmington in the summer. She arrived at Logan Airport wearing her Japanese baseball jacket on top of several other layers, and the temperature was ninety-one degrees. Thrusting her belly forward as Lee came to greet her, Peggy exclaimed, "I'm pregnant!" They drove to the Back Bay. The Stones had arranged for Peggy to stay with Jim and Dina Rose, the friends whose adoption of Jacob the summer before had encouraged them to write to the Colombian agency. The Roses warned the Stones that their friendship with each other might be tested if Peggy stayed with them and eventually decided not to give up the baby—a choice that the Roses felt was still Peggy's to make. They were also uncomfortable having Peggy with them under false pretenses and said that, if Peggy's parents ever asked them directly what she was really doing in Boston, they would tell the truth. Because of the Roses' affection for the Stones, they expressed concern about the openness of the adoption. But they were eager to help their friends.

Lee and Dan had told Peggy that she should stay with the Roses only if she was at ease there. Peggy's first impression was that the Roses had the most beautiful home she had ever seen: a three-story Victorian brick townhouse furnished with antique, modern, and post-modern pieces and a collection of old and contemporary clocks. After Lee and Peggy arrived, Dina showed Peggy her room, and then, to break the ice, the three women played with Jacob. "I got down on the floor and picked at his toes," Peggy said, "which you do with little kids." She unpacked a white bunny for Dan and Lee to have for the new baby and some VCR tapes from Tom (*Winnie the Pooh, Mary Poppins*, and *Fantasia*). Dina said later, "I knew I had a friend when Lee came back and said, 'Peggy wants to know, Is it O.K. for her to do laundry and put your laundry in with hers?' "

That night, Lee and Dan took Peggy out for dinner and a tour of Boston. She talked about Tom a lot and phoned him from a Thai restaurant where they ate. The Stones took her out for dinner the next night, too. The following day (Friday, June 24), as they had told Peggy they were going to do, they left for fifteen days of fieldwork in the West and the Northwest. They phoned Peggy from Flagstaff, Arizona, on Sunday, but then, while they were moving between locations in British Columbia, Alaska, and Montana, they didn't call again for two weeks. Dan explained, "The work was very hard, very absorbing, very compelling, and there was also the pleasure of being off together alone, and not having to deal with the real world. It was fun. I think we were a little irresponsible, in fact."

In Boston, Peggy settled into a routine. During the morning, after Jim headed off to work at his law firm, Peggy and Jacob often went to a playground, leaving Dina free for projects of her own. In the afternoon, Jacob stayed with Dina while Peggy put on a backpack and walked around the city. She liked to hang out on Washington Street, near the entrance to the discount basement in Filene's department store. It reminded her of Wilmington. If she didn't feel well, Peggy stayed in and napped. Several times, Peggy went out to the Jewish Family Service, in Framingham, to meet with a social worker. Most

nights, after Jacob went to sleep, she and the Roses ate together. "It really was bizarre what a comfortable little arrangement it was," Jim said.

Toward the start of July, Peggy met Colleen Rule, a midwife and a friend of the Stones. Colleen had encouraged the
Stones to think about adopting, and when they got back from
meeting Peggy and Tom in Washington, Lee asked Colleen if
she would take Peggy as a patient. Colleen explained, "I said
yes, and afterward I was scared. I said, 'Am I too much into
this?' " Colleen talked over the choice with a couple of colleagues and decided it was all right to do it: "I told Peggy that
Lee and Dan were my friends, which she already knew, but
that that had nothing now to do with our relationship, and
that nothing she ever said in my office would ever go outside the office unless she wished it to. I saw that Lee was
very right in her assessment of this girl. She was an incredibly
put-together twenty-year-old and had really thought things
through."

Lee and Dan got back on July 9, and a couple of days later
they came over to the Roses' house for a reunion and pizza.
Peggy made an announcement: her due date had been moved
up two weeks, to August 16. She also gave Lee and Dan their
first inkling that, despite her composed exterior, she had sometimes been struggling in Boston. As she had done in Washington the month before, Peggy launched into a monologue.
At first, the others tried to turn it into a conversation, but
Peggy seemed to need to get things off her chest. In contrast
to what she had told Dan when they first spoke by phone,
she said that she did not want to go on welfare to help cover
the costs of her stay in Boston. The Massachusetts Department
of Public Welfare required that, to qualify for state aid, she
must say she was keeping the baby, she had learned, and she
didn't want to tell a lie. She had been a hall monitor in ele-
mentary school, she said, and couldn't stand doing anything
wrong. Besides, she was afraid of creating a record that might
find its way to her parents and tip them off about her preg-

nancy. She also shared some of her fantasies about the baby. One was: "This baby will come see me, and will be really disappointed, because I won't be as great as it imagined." Mostly, she complained about the social worker assigned to her at the Jewish Family Service, calling her the "social worker from hell."

Jim was uncomfortable with this monologue, but barely spoke. As Peggy got worked up, Dina thought she sounded nervous and mechanical. Lee didn't know whether to express support for Peggy, to ask neutral questions, or to keep quiet. The silence of Peggy's audience unnerved Lee, however, and she found herself playing Peggy's chorus as Peggy attacked the social worker. Dan was troubled by what he heard, but held his tongue. "I watched this person say a lot of things that were very disturbing," he said. "Under ordinary circumstances, I would ask some questions and try to straighten it out and help in whatever way I could. In this situation, I didn't think it was my role to try to put her in touch with her feelings, in the way I might with a friend."

Peggy's social worker was Elayna Kirschtel, a twenty-seven-year-old with a master's degree from Rutgers University who had been with the Jewish Family Service for ten months when Peggy became her client. Kirschtel's previous experience had been as a counselor to the elderly and to troubled families for two and a half years and in an adoption internship during graduate school. She is conscientious and even-tempered, and she found Peggy intelligent, determined, and expressive. Peggy told the social worker how lonely and unsupported she had felt back home, as a result of her decision not to tell her family, and obliquely communicated a sense of shame about being pregnant. "Peggy was the good child," Kirschtel said later. "All of a sudden, she did this bad thing. She would never say that, but it seemed that way." Occasionally, Peggy would let her guard down with the social worker, weep inconsolably, and then seem unreachable while she rebuilt her defenses. "Peggy was fully armored," Kirschtel observed, "and she donned her armor for a specific reason. Everything she did seemed to be measured against the standard of what would be best for the baby. She had really thought through this process. My concern was that her plan was so rigid."

Kirschtel's approach to Peggy's case reflected the views of her boss, Paul Dubroff. He had approved of the Washington meeting between the Stones and Peggy and Tom, and after that, advised the Stones that they have no more contact with the birth mother. When Lee told Dubroff that she was picking Peggy up at the airport, he told her it was time for Lee and Dan to separate from her. Lee thought: Separate! We've only met this woman once for four hours! Dan called Diane Michelsen for a second opinion, and she advised them to do what they wanted. If you trust, you get trusted back, she said.

Dubroff's view was determined by a major and some minor concerns. He wanted to protect what he called the "integrity of the surrender," meaning Peggy's eventual decision to place the baby for adoption. By Massachusetts law, she couldn't sign papers surrendering the baby until ninety-six hours after the birth. Dubroff felt it was his job to protect her from any kind of inducement to give up the baby, including the cocoon-like pleasures of a temporary or even false friendship with Lee and Dan. He also had their interests in mind. The Jewish Family Service had taken part in one potential open adoption before theirs. During the last months of the pregnancy, the birth mother had lived with the prospective adopters, and the three had grown very close. When the birth mother changed her mind and kept the baby, Dubroff said later, the couple were devastated.

Peggy said, "Coercion was a major thing for them—that I would feel I owed it to Dan and Lee to give them the baby. Tom and I felt that was ridiculous, because we didn't feel we owed it to Dan and Lee. It was Dan and Lee's baby. We had picked them. It wasn't, 'Gee, they took me to the movies, I'll have to give them my firstborn child!' It wasn't that kind of situation." Peggy scorned each of the ways the agency was concerned that Lee and Dan might sway her ("If they had crossed my palm with gold," she said about a key one, "that would have been it") and especially put down Elayna's role. "Elayna was basically a textbook social worker," she said. "It was a joke with Dan and Lee and me, 'Can we work up some grief here so Elayna will feel like she's social working?' The whole denial process: she would ask me, 'Are you denying that you're giving up the baby?' I was *living* with it *every day*."

The day after the reunion over pizza, on July 12, the Massachusetts Office for Children held a one-day hearing about amending its regulations on licensing adoption agencies. Among other topics, the hearing addressed proposed new limits on the amount of financial help that agencies (and prospective adopters) could give birth mothers for expenses related to adoptions. The practices of some private agencies in the state (meeting birth mothers at the airport in limousines, helping them pay for college tuition) had drawn the spotlight to gray-market adoptions: not black-market deals or outright baby-selling, but arrangements that could be described as ethically ambiguous. Dina Rose attended the hearing and was especially touched by the testimony of a birth mother who sat next to the witness table while someone else read her statement. For Dina, the lesson of the day was that, wherever a birth mother lived during her pregnancy, she had to feel supported and cared for, and free to keep or give up the baby after the birth.

Dina discussed the hearing with Jim and the next morning made a speech to Peggy. The gist of it was that, while she respected Peggy's reasons for planning to give the baby to Lee and Dan, she recognized that she and Jim had a conflict of interest: they were housing the birth mother but clearly wanted the baby to go to their friends. Dina said, "It is important for me that you know you are completely free to change your mind at any time, and that you are under no obligation whatsoever, not only not to Dan and Lee but not to us, either, to go through with this adoption." Peggy's eyes filled with tears.

Through the rest of July, Lee and Dan saw Peggy about

once a week. They had dinner together and went to the movies; she called them when she had technical questions about adoption that the Jewish Family Service couldn't answer. Dan went away the latter part of the month for ten days of fieldwork, and Lee left Boston at the same time for a long weekend. The Roses were Peggy's anchor. Peggy made Elayna a regular topic of conversation with them. Jim said that Elayna and Peggy sounded like a mismatch: the social worker was asking all the right questions but was irritating the birth mother. Peggy also seemed to be provoking Elayna: reenacting one session, Peggy had herself looking at her watch during their meetings, to signal that she had reached her limit.

As far as the Roses could tell, Peggy never reconsidered her decision to give up the baby. One reason, Dina decided, was that Peggy was a person of her word. For Jim, there was a more telling explanation. Peggy's relationship to Lee and Dan—the phone calls, the meeting in Washington, their small world in Boston—had a distorted, hazy quality, a kind of buzz. Jim thought the birth mother and the prospective adopters were falling in love.

Dan: "Peggy went this tremendous length in making us feel like parents and putting us in touch with issues and making us think about what mattered to us in this really amazing and gentle and wonderful way. It made her feel great to have us feel excited for her pregnancy. We could experience the pregnancy of our child, and she could experience the pleasure of being pregnant because it was our child. It was the perfect match—not something that we even fantasized about, something that she constructed and that we were very happy to go along with."

One of the provisions Peggy made for Lee and Dan was that they be with her for the birth. The midwife, Colleen Rule, initially vetoed the idea. Her main objection was that Lee, as a prenatal nurse, would be too preoccupied with the details of delivery. ("I thought Lee would watch the fetal monitor and, every time it dipped, would go, 'Oh, my God, my kid's I.Q. just fell another couple of points.' ") She was also opposed because at the hospital where she worked no adoptive parents had ever been with a birth mother at birth.

Soon after Peggy became her patient, another longtime patient came to see Colleen. The woman had three children of her own and, the year before, had given birth to a fourth child whom she had relinquished to infertile friends in New York State. When Colleen mentioned Peggy's proposal to her, this woman thought it was a fine idea. The adoptive mother had been with her at the New York birth: that made her feel that she was really the baby's mother and relieved the birth mother of the sense she had to respond to the baby's every need. The woman was pregnant again, with a baby for some friends in Washington State, and this time both the adoptive mother and father were going to be with her at the birth. "I got a totally inside scoop," Colleen said, and she changed her mind.

On August 2, Lee and Dan learned about another provision Peggy had made for them. Peggy's due date was approaching and the three felt the need to do some preparation for the birth. They felt awkward going to a class for couples, so they arranged for a private tutorial with a nurse. The teacher started with the female anatomy and how it changed during a pregnancy. Peggy acted cute and precocious, showing off what she had already learned. The teacher taught some breathing techniques for Peggy to use during labor contractions, and all three practiced them. Peggy announced that she was going to give birth naturally—no anesthesia; squatting for delivery; chanting a mantra to distract herself from the pain.

Peggy found it endearing that Dan took the class so seriously, and was surprised at how little he knew about childbirth—for example, he didn't know the uterus is a muscle. In the meantime, Dan and Lee were trying to hide how overwhelmed they were by emotions loosed during the class.

Dan: "Here we were spending all our time with this pregnant woman, and it was wonderful, and yet this was the first time we were walking into the belly of the monster. A little blithely, I thought we could take anything. It was somehow like we were giving birth. This was the first time it was obvious—we weren't."

Lee: "I thought, I should be doing this. Tears just streamed out. It wasn't my experience."

The nurse asked, "After the baby is born, it's going to go to you, Lee?" Lee said, "No, it's going to Peggy." The nurse looked from one woman to the other. "No, it's going to Lee," Peggy said. "I've already signed the paper." Peggy said she wanted the baby to go to Lee first, because she wanted the baby's first smell to be of its mother.

Lee: "I had this image of taking a kitten from its mother, and I thought of how horrible that is. I couldn't get that out of my head."

The Roses went away for three weeks' vacation on August 6. Peggy continued to stay at their house, but she and the Stones were now together almost every day. "Things got very obscure, because of the intensity we felt for her," Lee said.

Dan: "Whatever kinds of worries we had about being close, all that went out the window. There was no choice at this point. We were involved enough to be concerned about her as a person. She had nobody else in town."

Lee: "We wanted to provide for her and take care of her. I wasn't making the connection that she was giving us this baby."

Around August 8, Miriam Cato, a woman in Lee's mind-body group, asked if she could meet Peggy. Dan was strongly against the meeting. It made sense for him and Lee to know Peggy, because they were going to be the adoptive parents. It made sense for the Roses to know her, because they had housed her. But Peggy was not going to be a regular part of the lives of any of them, and any meetings between her and other friends would have a voyeuristic quality. "Checking out the genes," they called it. Lee agreed, and they didn't raise the subject with Peggy.

One night soon after, Peggy came to dinner at Lee and Dan's. It was the first time Peggy had been to their house, and she said she loved it. The Stones lived in a large three-bedroom condominium in a red brick building on a quiet street near Coolidge Corner, in Brookline. The condo was a relaxed, orderly showplace for various serious, goofy, and lovely finds: antique porcelain plates; foreign soapboxes; postcards with scenes from the nineteen-fifties; and lots of kitsch. On the sill above the kitchen sink were families of Carrot people, penguins, Gumby dolls, and Conehead candles. Nearby was a quartet of red plastic Esso penny banks and, hanging on a wall one above the other, a couple of cat clocks with tails and eyes that ticked like metronomes. The Stones slept on a futon next to a fireplace, in part of a double living room that was filled with fine pieces of antique wooden furniture. The most trafficked room was the kitchen, which had a soft couch under a large window in one corner, a kilim rug on a natural oak floor, and, on a wall of exposed brick, an outline of the Rocky Mountains in white neon.

The three arrived together, and Lee flipped on the telephone-answering machine to listen to messages. Miriam Cato said on the machine, "Lee, I hope Dan has changed his mind about Peggy." Lee turned the machine off. Peggy looked bewildered. To all of them, the message had said that Dan was having second thoughts about Peggy as their birth mother. He felt obliged to explain. "Miriam wanted to meet you, and we didn't want to put you through this, and I wasn't sure I wanted to do this with our friends," he said. "How do you feel about it?"

Peggy said she was eager: "If I can help any of your friends, by all means." Continuing her effort to prepare Lee and Dan for their child, she also asked what last name they planned to give the baby: Stone? Duncan-Stone? They didn't know.

On Wednesday, August 10, the three went to an educational movie called *Labors of Love*, whose opening scenes showed four couples with new babies, graphic pictures of labor, and then couples embracing. "I don't think that there is anything like it in the world," one new mother said in the movie. "I always knew that childbirth was a really magnificent thing . . . But until you go through it yourself, I don't think there's really a way to describe it to someone else." The movie made Lee and Dan feel excluded by depicting an experience they couldn't have, and made Peggy feel lonely and frightened. The three left early.

Saturday, the 13th, Lee and Peggy had brunch with Miriam Cato. Miriam: "I was so nervous. I didn't know what I wanted her to be. I didn't believe she was doing this: that you could go through a summer like this, and stay with friends of the couple to whom you were going to give your baby, and give them your baby. Peggy said she felt wonderful doing this. She wished she could be in charge of this sort of thing to counsel other birth mothers. She said, 'I would do it for *you*. Someone will do it for you.'"

Lee said later, "Miriam started sobbing, I started sobbing, and Peggy started sobbing, and Peggy said, 'Would you girls stop it! I don't want to sob!' We were total basket cases, and here was Peggy talking about why pregnancy wasn't that big a deal. Miriam and I were kicking each other under the table, and pinching our thighs."

Driving away, Peggy said to Lee, "I'm the adoption fairy!"

Birth

Peggy often felt sick and heavy in Boston, and she was regularly bothered by the heat. (The daily high temperature in August was rarely below ninety, and both the city and the state issued warnings against going outside unless it was truly necessary.) The coolest place to spend the days was at the movies, and the Stones and she went often. On the 13th, Dan's older brother, Aaron, arrived from California to lend support. At Dan's suggestion and with Peggy's gratitude, Aaron moved into the Roses', to keep her company. On the 15th, Lee and Dan didn't see Peggy, and on the 16th, Peggy's due date, Lee and Peggy went to look at some paintings at the Sackler Museum, at Harvard. Then they went to a cookout with Dan and Aaron at the house of some of their relatives who had a swimming pool, where Peggy floated unabashedly, belly up.

On the 17th, Peggy thought that she was going into labor. She reached Dan at his office to let him know, and he was out the door in seconds. It was a false alarm. The midwife had told Peggy to come in for a checkup if she started having contractions every ten minutes, and Lee had noticed that their punctual arrival seemed to be determined by Peggy's close attention to the clock. Peggy's spirits plummeted. She wanted to go home. School would start in two weeks, she said, and the delay in the birth might get her caught. Thursday the 18th was another day of frustration for Peggy. Friday, she asked to be left alone.

On Saturday, the 20th, the four sat around the Roses' bedroom with the air conditioner on, kidding each other and passing the time. Peggy watched a videotape of the movie *Manhunter*; she had half jokingly chosen its theme song by the heavy-metal group Iron Butterfly as the theme music for the birth. She spoke about her family, saying she had told them she was serving as the labor coach for the impending delivery of a pregnant friend. When Lee and Aaron went downstairs to make dinner, Dan said there was something important he wanted to talk about. He asked Peggy if she had thought about the kind of contact she would like to have with him and Lee after the birth. Peggy said she wanted them to do whatever they thought was right. The kind of contact they should have was a "parental call." She went on to say something different from what she and Tom had said in Washington. She would understand if they cut off contact with her, Peggy said, but if they were willing she wanted to stay in touch and know as much as possible about the baby.

Lee rejoined them and empathized with Peggy as a mother losing her child. "One of the painful parts of the adoption is that the baby didn't come out of Agency Heaven," Dan said later. "It didn't drop from the sky. There's not this anonymous woman out there, but this flesh-and-blood person we have tremendous affection for, losing her child. At one and the same time, we experience her grief and her appreciation for how good the situation is. Things go side by side. And this was the first time we saw the other side of it, because we were all very intent on keeping it good. This relationship, with all its vagaries and necessities, was starting to fray a little bit."

After dinner, Peggy spoke at length about how she was really loved, and asked Dan and Lee to read some personal letters she had received. One was a romantic letter from Tom, delivered that afternoon by Federal Express. The others were from her mother and father and her grandparents, to their "little Raggedy Ann." A note from her father included some drawings by him. Peggy said that she planned to give the baby a painting her father had made for her, with a single bristle, when she was a little girl. Lee considered Peggy's invitation to read the letters an act of intimacy. Dan thought it was a sign of deep loneliness.

On Sunday, the 21st, Dan came by the Roses' to make a movie of Peggy talking straight at the camera: she hadn't expected him yet and had just finished ordering an anchovy pizza. In the movie, she is sitting next to a window in the Roses' bedroom, wearing a floral-print maternity dress. The light is soft and makes her skin look creamy. Her hands, touching her stomach, appear exquisite: strong fingers, with a rose-hued polish on her nails. Her glasses keep slipping down her nose, and she pushes them back with the index finger of her right hand. At first, Peggy is giggly and a little schoolmarmish, making weak jokes about her next pregnancy. Then she speculates about what the baby she is carrying will look like. ("I keep thinking it could have all my features and look really good. Or it could have all of Tom's features, and if it's a girl, it could look really funny.") Dan says the baby will be wonderful-looking, and Peggy is dismissive.

Dan asks if Peggy knows why she chose him and Lee to be the parents of her baby.

"Just when I heard your names, it sounded right," she says.

Dan goes on, "Funny. The names themselves. Did they tell you much about us?"

Peggy: "Not a whole lot. I didn't want to know a whole lot. I knew you were it."

Dan says, "It's been great for us knowing you. What's it been like for you?"

Peggy: "God, it's been, like, the worst experience of my entire life to know the parents of . . . Lee keeps saying what a wonderful thing I'm doing. *You're* giving *me* a lifetime of security knowing that my baby is going to be taken care of by its parents. I mean, what else can I ask for?"

Dan says, "Well, we're in love with this child."

Peggy: "That's all that's important. That's all Tom and I care about. That's everything." And: "Here I am getting all choked up about how wonderful I am. It's just important to me that the baby has what you guys are going to give it . . . I know that I probably would have given this baby less emotionally than you guys will, because it's not supposed to be mine. It's supposed to be your guys. I know everybody keeps saying it's an impossible thing to know, but it's not. Maybe it's impossible for everybody else, but not for me. That's just the way it goes."

Peggy went to see Colleen the first thing the next morning. Colleen had agreed to make a final effort to help Peggy's labor begin more or less naturally. She put on surgical gloves, moistened them with a water-soluble jelly called Lubrifax, and then ran her fingers between Peggy's cervix and the membranes surrounding the baby, to stimulate the uterus to contract. The procedure was quite uncomfortable and, apparently, unsuccessful.

Afterward, Lee, Dan, and Aaron took Peggy shopping, and walking around Harvard Square, Peggy said, "Guys, I think my membranes are ruptured!" She and Lee found a bathroom in the Square. Peggy was very nervous. She checked herself, and she said, "Yup, I'm really bleeding!" The nurse in Lee asked Peggy to show her what she had found. Peggy was soaking wet from the Lubrifax, but the blood Peggy displayed was old and brown. For Peggy's sake, the four drove to the Roses' and called Colleen. They were told to monitor her and, if she showed signs of labor, to bring her in.

In the late afternoon, Peggy felt more contractions. Her description was persuasive, and Lee and Dan drove her to the hospital. Peggy was officially admitted, a nurse put an identifying bracelet on her, she was hooked up to a fetal monitor, and she was prepared for delivery. The nurse gave her a litmus test to see if her membranes were ruptured, and it was negative. One of Colleen's colleagues (Colleen had gone off duty) gave Peggy another test to confirm her status: she extracted some fluid from her vagina with a syringe and looked at it through a microscope to see if there was a pattern called ferning, which is another indicator for amniotic fluid. The test was negative.

While Peggy was waiting for the results, a hospital social worker came to visit her. She asked the same question that the Jewish Family Service had posed repeatedly: Was Peggy sure she wanted to give up the baby? The news that she wasn't in labor disappointed Peggy, and she felt ambushed by the social worker. She could barely talk. "Look, we just had a dress rehearsal," Lee told her. "Tomorrow's gonna be the day." The Stones drove Peggy and Aaron back to the Roses' for the night.

At a quarter to seven the next morning, Lee and Dan picked up Peggy and Aaron, to get Peggy to the hospital shortly after seven. Colleen gave Peggy what she considered the hospital's best birthing room: it had Laura Ashley wallpaper (white flowers on a blue background) and a wooden rocking chair next to the bed. Peggy's membranes were ruptured with a sterile instrument resembling a crochet hook, and through an intravenous tube she was given a synthetic hormone called Pitocin, to induce labor. By 9:30, Peggy began to feel contractions, and she was chirpy.

"We were a wreck," Dan said. "There was this incredible sense of anticipation, and there was lots of stuff going on that we weren't party to. In some ways, it was like the father's role in the classic situation. We were downstairs a good part of the morning drinking coffee, and just waiting and not knowing what was going on."

In the late morning, Peggy fell asleep. Dan went to get some exercise. Lee and Aaron took a long walk along the Charles

River. Lee, generally a vegetarian, ate two hot dogs. When Lee and Dan returned to Peggy's room, she was asleep but was having mild contractions. Her wrists were crossed, and she was whimpering from the pain. Lee and Dan were taken aback by the change in her condition, and Colleen asked them to leave again.

Around one o'clock, Lee and the nurse on duty, Laura Cahill, suggested that Peggy be given an epidural anesthetic to ease her pain. Peggy had already asked Colleen for a dose, and after it was administered, she asked that Lee and Dan come see her again, to assure them that she was O.K. They talked for a while, Lee and Dan squeezed her hand, and Peggy nodded off.

Not long after, Colleen took Lee and Dan aside. She said, "I feel as if I haven't had any time to address your needs today and you haven't had any time to address your own needs. Now that Peggy isn't going to have any more pain, what are your thoughts?" Lee asked, "Will I know what to do when the baby is born?" Colleen laughed, and answered, "Definitely."

At around 4:30 that afternoon, the doctors and the midwives on duty reviewed the status of their current patients on evening rounds. In case something went wrong with Peggy's delivery and she needed care from a doctor, Colleen decided to alert the group to the unusual circumstances of the birth. She presented the case: "This is Margaret Bass. She's forty-one weeks pregnant. Her cervix is seven centimeters dilated; the fetal heart tracing is good. Everything is fine. I anticipate a normal delivery without problems, and, by the way, this woman is involved in an open adoption and the adoptive parents are with her."

One of the doctors snapped, "That's not allowed."

Colleen asked, "Which rule are you talking about? Don't you think you're just a little uncomfortable personally with this?" The doctor backed off.

At 5:15, Colleen examined Peggy and said to Lee and Dan,

"Put on your scrub suits. You're going to be parents soon."
To give Peggy the privacy she had asked for, Colleen stationed
Dan at Peggy's head, to rub her shoulders occasionally, and
Lee next to her left leg. Laura and Colleen each held one of
Peggy's legs as she lay on her back. For some reason, although
Lee knew that the final steps of labor can take two hours, she
thought it was going to be over in minutes. It took an hour
and fifty-three minutes.

With Peggy's permission, Lee and Dan made an audiotape
of the delivery. The final minute went:

Peggy: "Here it is! It's moving its face. It's tickling! Ahhh.
O.K."

Colleen: "We're almost there, darling!"

Peggy: [The baby's head is out. Peggy reaches down and
feels the head]: "It feels like it's trying to talk. Oh, my God!"

Dan: "Doin' good, doin' good."

Peggy: "Oh, it's adorable!"

Lee: "Oh, look at its little hair. Hello, pumpkin."

Dan: "Look at her . . ."

Laura: "Big deep breath, and go again!"

Colleen: "Beautiful, beautiful, what control, what control..."

Peggy: "Can you see its eyes opening?"

Colleen: "You can see its eyes and—"

Peggy: "It's got Tom's head."

Lee: "Didn't get your head, Peggy. It got Tom's egghead."

Peggy: "Oh, my God, it's moving really hard!"

Laura: "Holy shit, go!"

Peggy: "Holy shit?"

Laura: "It's just the baby's about out!"

Colleen: "O.K., take a rest."

Peggy: "How can I rest when I've got someone gumming
my pelvis from the inside?"

Colleen: "There's a point."

Lee: "It's got your lips. It's little Peggy!"

Laura: "Ohhh" [a whisper, as the baby rotates its shoulders
and pops out] "that's it."

Peggy: "Tom's shoulders, guys."

Lee: "She's a beautiful girl. Oh, yesss. You're a *beautiful* girl . . ."

Colleen: "Who would like to cut the cord?" [The baby cries] "Dan?"

Dan: "Yes." [Struggling] "That's harder than I thought."

Lee: "Peggy." [Walking over to give her a kiss] "Oh, *yeah*."

Lee and Dan announced that they would call the baby Rebecca Duncan Stone, and a nurse took some pictures: Dan holding Lee's arm, Lee standing next to Peggy, and Peggy holding the bedrail; Peggy holding Rebecca while Lee, Dan, and Aaron drank some champagne from Dixie cups; Lee, behind a curtain, gazing closely at Rebecca; Peggy, without her glasses, swaddling Rebecca; Peggy sitting at the head of the bed drinking a Coke, and gazing at the Stones, at the foot of the bed, as they huddled around Rebecca.

"I think she was very happy how out to lunch we were," Dan said not long after. "And I think that was maybe the first time in which Peggy felt that she'd done O.K., that she'd made the right decision and that we would love Rebecca."

A few minutes after the birth, Peggy called Tom. "Yes, I think I'm very satisfied with what we produced," Peggy said. "She's got a really squished puppy little face." In the background, Lee agreed with her. "She has very dark eyes," Peggy said. "Very pretty eyes," Dan said. "Very pretty eyes," Lee repeated, as she held the baby. Peggy went on, "I don't know how much she weighs." The baby cried and Peggy said, "This little person is going to be sound asleep. I spent most of the day sound asleep. Dan and Lee were the ones who were running around."

Lee said, "Yeah, right, we did so much."

Lee and Dan called the Roses and some other friends, and Lee and Peggy called Miriam Cato. "I gave the baby to the mother and father," Peggy said. "Hey, if you ever end up in this position, you'd better have a spinal. If you get pregnant, which I hope you do, forget all this natural stuff."

Lee moved to the rocking chair at the foot of the bed, still holding Rebecca, and Peggy was illuminated by a small light behind her head. Later, Dan remembered her as seeming regal. A photograph shows her looking exhausted. Peggy said, "She's tasting the smell of you, Lee." Rebecca cried for a while, and Peggy said of the adoption, "You guys should get a finalization on her not long after Valentine's Day." She went on, "Now she has to meet Jacob. Don't let him smack her."

Lee was absorbed in Rebecca. "That little toe," she said. "You're perfect, your toes are perfect, you're perfect." Dan added, "Your gums are perfect."

Assessing Rebecca's condition one minute and five minutes after birth, Colleen Rule had given her high ratings on the Apgar scale. Lee said, "And you're already going to be conceited, because you made a 9/9 on your Apgar."

Peggy: "I am so impressed with myself."

To Lee, Dan said, "You're a Mom."

To Rebecca, Lee said, "We waited for you for a long time."

Rebecca cried again and Peggy said, "Hey, that's enough. Not many kids get to pick their parents."

At eight, a voice over the public-address system announced that visiting hours were over. Lee and Dan had been warned that they might have trouble moving freely around the hospital, since they had no legal tie to Rebecca yet and no credentials for staying after hours, but they wanted to go with the baby to the postpartum floor. They tagged along as the nurse took Rebecca to the nursery, and Lee and Dan watched her through the window. A woman who had just given birth came by to check on her own baby. She noticed Rebecca, asked how old she was, and said, "Who's the mother?" Lee thought, We'll have to get used to this, and said, "I am." The woman sized up Lee and said, "You ain't the mother! You can't be the mother! You look too good!"

On the way out of the hospital, Lee and Dan remarked

about one of the birth's surprises: sometime during the summer, after they had decided how much they liked Peggy's hair and wanted their baby to be a redhead, they told her the story about how Lee had blacklisted the color before they met her. Peggy trumped them by confessing that she was only a redhead à l'Oréal: she had been dyeing her hair since she was ten, and couldn't pass the color on. Rebecca was a redhead.

When Lee and Dan got home, there was a message on the answering machine for their cat: "Hello, Otis, this is Peggy. And I'm just calling to let you know it was a baby girl, and I'm very, very fond of it and you're going to have to be extra-nice to it. You're gonna have to be extra-nice to them, too, because they look pretty beat, so I'm gonna need you to take care of them tonight, so when they come and bring the baby tomorrow you have the situation under control. And I'm really counting on you for this, Otie, O.K.? Be good, and I'll talk to you later."

An unspoken rule observed by Peggy and the Stones from the day she arrived in Boston seemed to be that she wouldn't tell them about the grief she felt at the prospect of giving up her baby and they wouldn't talk with her about their fears that she would change her mind or about the pain of their infertility.

After Peggy's meetings with Elayna, she often called Tom and cried to him. "It wasn't really fair to him, but I didn't want to cry to Dan and Lee and I didn't want to blubber at Dina and Jim," she said. A few times, Peggy cried when she was with Jacob: "He would come up and pat me on the back. When you're feeling really down and gross, that makes you feel even worse." She grew tired of talk about babies, of being treated as if she were ten years older than she was, of anything to do with children. She worried that she would be jealous of her friends who had children, and toward the end of her pregnancy, when she regularly felt sick, she thought she never wanted to be pregnant again.

When Lee and Dan weren't with Peggy, they talked about her often. Some of the talk was about how she was preparing them to be parents. A lot was about their affection and respect for her. But when Peggy revealed a sign of distress, they recoiled. Peggy's neediness brought out their own. Her monologue in early July was particularly unsettling, and there were similar moments when they asked themselves if Peggy was having second thoughts.

One upsetting subject that the Stones and Peggy did talk about was money. Both couples (Tom along with Peggy) were dissatisfied with how the Jewish Family Service had handled the financial side of the adoption. The Massachusetts adoption climate that had led to the July hearing about amending state adoption regulations had made the Family Service particularly intent on following current law so that the adoptions it supervised would be above criticism. For Peggy, a major frustration was that the pregnancy was costing her a summer's work, and under its reading of Massachusetts law the Family Service believed it could not make up for her lost wages out of funds it held in escrow from the Stones to cover her expenses. (If the adoption had taken place in California, it would have been acceptable for the Stones to give Peggy as much as five thousand dollars—for relocation, for example.) Peggy was also upset that the agency would not reimburse her for the cost of doctors' visits she told them she made in Wilmington before coming to Boston, for the meals she had paid for, or for clothes she had bought to hide her expanding girth. She was told she would receive payment for any legitimate past expense that she could document with receipts, and this seemed to her unfair. In her view, the expenses she had incurred in Wilmington were a fraction of what Lee's would have been in Boston if Lee had been pregnant. The amount that would have satisfied Peggy for meals and doctor's visits, she said not long after, was $1,700.

For prospective adopters, the Jewish Family Service had a sliding scale of fees. The Stones' combined income was more than $30,000, so they paid the agency's top fee of $5,750.

Adoption agencies sometimes justify their fees by citing the costs of matching birth mothers with prospective adopters and caring for the birth mothers during pregnancy. Since Diane Michelsen had introduced Peggy to the Stones (she charged them $1,361.29, including $171.50 for their share of the cost of several classified ads), they thought their fee should cover only the cost of their home study, the cost of counseling for Peggy, and any post-adoption services. They liked the social worker assigned to them but, especially after Peggy's counseling seemed to prove ineffectual, wondered why the fee was so high. Aside from the basic fee, they had also deposited with the agency more than five thousand dollars to cover Peggy's medical, housing, and other expenses, and couldn't understand why the agency wasn't reimbursing Peggy for at least some of the expenses that she claimed.

The Jewish Family Service increased the Stones' dissatisfaction when it sent them a form letter at the end of July that reflected the agency's sense of priorities in the new era of adoption, to serve what Paul Dubroff called "more balanced interests." It stated that "once a child is legally surrendered to this Agency, it is the sole responsibility of the Agency to determine the placement of the baby; however, you will be given first consideration as the prospective adoptive parents for the child." It also said, "We would like you to know that while the Agency provides the required adoption services in your behalf, the Agency does not serve as your agent. At whatever time the birth parent(s) becomes a client of this Agency, the Agency serves as agent for the biological parent(s) and the child."

The effect of the letter, together with Peggy's displeasure over the agency's counseling, was that neither she nor the Stones viewed the Jewish Family Service as a satisfactory advocate. In the days before the birth, the agency asked Peggy, Lee, and Dan where they wanted the baby to go immediately after the hospital; in the process of negotiating an answer before the birth, the agency gave Peggy and the Stones more reason to feel left on their own. There were three choices: the baby could go to the Roses' with Peggy; the baby could go into foster care until Peggy signed the adoption papers; or she could go home with the Stones. Hospital policy was that the baby could not stay there. The Stones wanted the baby with them, and Peggy adamantly agreed—the baby should be with her parents.

The Family Service wavered. By law, Peggy wasn't allowed to sign the adoption papers until four full days after the birth (until 7:08 p.m., on Saturday, August 27); the staff wanted to protect the Stones from the pain of having the baby taken away from them if Peggy decided not to give up the baby. (Since the end of the four days would fall late on Saturday, the Jewish Family Service planned to hold a signing on Monday morning.) There was also the "integrity of the surrender": Peggy's awareness that she would hurt the Stones if she took the baby back from them might be seen as a possible form of coercion to relinquish the child. Peggy decided that the best solution was to say she wanted the baby with her and then for her to give the baby to the Stones. If the agency called Peggy to see how things were going, she would cover for them. Lee and Dan decided that it was wrong to take part in a charade that could jeopardize the adoption, and when they told the agency about their intention of taking the baby home, the plan seemed directly at odds with Peggy's. More phone calls straightened things out so the baby could go home with the Stones, but everyone's nerves were frayed.

Paul Dubroff commented, "We serve the best interests of the child first, the birth mother next, and we don't represent the adoptive couple. We very often develop a very tight bond with the adoptive couple and sometimes people have an enormous need to blur who we represent."

On the way to the hospital the day after the birth, Lee said to Dan, "I really hope Peggy calls the baby Rebecca." When they walked into Peggy's room, Peggy said, "Rebecca, Rebecca—your mom and dad are here. Go to your mom and dad." They were reassured, but noticed that the name tag on the baby's crib, on which had been printed "Rebecca Duncan Stone" (Peggy had already taken the unusual step of putting the name that the Stones gave the baby on her original birth certificate), had been replaced by one marked "Baby Girl Bass." Lee and Dan spent part of the day visiting with Peggy and Rebecca, taking turns giving formula to the baby. As if she were a nanny, Peggy kept a distance from Rebecca, and giggled happily when Dan put a diaper on backward the first time he changed the baby. As Dan and Lee were leaving, Peggy asked, "So who's coming back for the night feeding?" They appreciated Peggy's insistence that they act like parents. They also noticed that, instead of staying in the nursery, the baby was rooming in with Peggy.

On Thursday, when Lee and Dan returned to the hospital to pick up Rebecca, Peggy was talking to Elayna. The door was shut. Lee and Dan thought to themselves, What if Elayna says, "You guys, she just can't do it"? Half an hour passed before Elayna joined them. Walking down the hall toward Lee and Dan, Elayna kept a poker face.

"Everything is fine, but Peggy is upset about money," she said. Peggy was requesting $900 for meals in Wilmington and $1,400 for medical expenses. Again, Elayna had reminded her that unless she furnished receipts the agency couldn't reimburse her. The tension was relieved, Elayna said, when she promised to raise the matter one more time with Paul Dubroff.

Elayna did not tell the Stones the main reason Peggy was on edge. "Because of the reality of facing her family," Elayna said some time later. "She knew that the adoption was right, that she felt right about it. She knew Rebecca was going to be happy." But, to the social worker, Peggy's "real life" was starting again, and she was frightened. The feelings surfaced in a fantasy that by returning to Wilmington with an empty bank account she would tip off her parents about the adoption. Elayna had encouraged Peggy to tell them, and consult them, right away—once she surrendered the baby, Elayna pointed out, the decision would be considered final, although it would be some months before a judge approved the adoption. Peggy could put the baby in foster care, Elayna noted, fly home, and take things from there. (To herself, Elayna thought that if Peggy took her advice the Jewish Family Service probably wouldn't let her leave the baby with the Stones: the likelihood of her deciding to keep the baby would be too great.) Peggy had rejected Elayna's counsel and stuck to her script.

Tom arrived Thursday afternoon to be with Peggy at the Roses', and Friday at nine o'clock he called to say they were ready to visit with Rebecca any time the Stones could bring her over. It was a modest but confusing change of plans: Peggy had said that she wanted Tom to spend time with the baby at the Stones' place. Lee and Dan decided they had no choice except to comply, and at 9:30 they brought Rebecca over, with a bottle of formula and one extra diaper—enough for about a two-hour visit. They left and waited for Peggy and Tom's call.

They didn't hear from Peggy and Tom for four hours. They turned on their answering machine and went out to do some errands, and when they got home, around three, almost six hours after leaving Rebecca off, there was still no message. Lee couldn't take the waiting and called the Roses' house. Tom said, "How come you guys didn't call?" Lee said, "Because we were waiting for you to call." Tom told her they had gone out and bought some more diapers and formula, and were playing rock and roll. "We'll call you later," he said, and hung up. Lee and Dan decided that there must have been a misunderstanding (after a while, Tom and Peggy did feel as if they were baby-sitting, they said later), and Dan called after a few minutes to say they would like to pick up Rebecca.

When the Stones arrived, Tom was prickly, and Peggy didn't come downstairs to see them. Tom handed Rebecca to Lee and said that he and Peggy were thinking of leaving on Sunday, before they were scheduled to sign the adoption papers. They weren't getting the money they expected from the Jewish Family Service, Tom said. Peggy was feeling pressure from her family to come home, he went on, and was angry at Paul Dubroff for sending her home broke, after not returning any of her calls. Also, Tom had just started a new job and didn't want to miss another day of work. He said that he and Peggy didn't want to do anything to jeopardize having Rebecca placed with Lee and Dan, but the message he conveyed was that he and Peggy felt mistreated, after all they had done.

On the Stones' answering machine at home, Elayna had left a message to call her right away. She didn't want to alarm them, she began, but Peggy and Tom had canceled a counseling session scheduled for that afternoon. She warned that it would be an unfortunate turn of events if Peggy and Tom left before signing the surrender. Delaware's adoption law was different from Massachusetts', and an early departure would put the adoption at risk. Dan worked the phones. By late morning on Saturday, he had persuaded the Jewish Family Service to let Peggy and Tom sign the papers on Sunday, in time to catch a plane home. Elayna found a notary public who could make the signing official. Dan called Tom to report the news.

"How's Lee?" Tom asked.

Dan replied, "It's like she's having a miscarriage."

Saturday night, Peggy and Lee spoke for the first time since Thursday afternoon, by phone. Peggy excused herself for staying upstairs the day before (her breasts were painfully engorged from not being used to feed the baby, she said), and declared that she had never meant to cause any anguish. "You've been so great, I love you so much, you've been so supportive, and I'll never forget you in the delivery room," she said. She then offered to have another baby for the Stones.

Sunday morning, some friends of the Stones drove Tom and Peggy to Elayna's house, out in the suburbs, and there they signed the papers formally bestowing Rebecca on the Stones. Paul Dubroff was in attendance to make sure everything was done properly. The Stones had been told by Dubroff that if they gave Peggy a ride and she later changed her mind about giving up the baby, she might be able to claim that she had been brainwashed on the way. Peggy and Tom seemed almost giddy and were clearly eager to go home. It occurred to Peggy, after Elayna interrupted the signing to ask, "Now you know this is final?" that Elayna might think they were being very casual about giving away their child.

The Case for Openness

The case for open adoption is now most often made in a series of accepted maxims: It enables birth mothers to resolve their guilt and grief about giving up their baby, since they know that the child is all right and that his adoptive parents care for him. It allows adoptive parents to replace fantasies about their child's background with accurate details, and to deal more honestly with themselves and their child about the adoption. Most important, it permits adoptees to come to terms with a basic element of their identity, since they know their biological roots and why their birth mother placed them for adoption, and they can move beyond the secrecy and the sense of rejection that can accompany conventional adoptions.

The evidence in support of these statements is in part anecdotal, but increasingly it is scholarly too. The new scholarly work concerns the psychological effects of adoption, in particular on adopted children. The Census Bureau reports that about five million American adoptees are now alive—about two percent of this country's population consists of adoptees. By contrast, adopted children make up about five percent of the outpatients and between ten and fifteen percent of the inpatients at mental-health facilities. According to Kent Ravenscroft, who teaches psychiatry at the Georgetown University School of Medicine and has reviewed these clinical studies, adoptees show aggression more often than nonadoptees do, have more feelings of rootlessness and low self-esteem, and have more learning problems. They are more likely to be depressed, to lie, steal, or run away, and to have trouble concentrating.

The explanation for these problems lies, in part, in nature: among other things, the birth mother is often a teenager whose poor prenatal care, use of drugs or alcohol during pregnancy, or complicated delivery exacts a continuing toll. But a prominent adoption scholar, D. M. Brodzinsky, of Rutgers University, contends that the cause for some, and perhaps many, of these problems can be traced to the adoption experience itself. "For adoptees, part of them is hurt at having once been relinquished," he observes. "That part remains vulnerable for the rest of their lives as they grieve at various predictable points for the unknown parents who gave them away."

The extreme expression of these problems, according to David Kirschner, a clinical psychologist, is the "adopted child syndrome," marked by rebellion, truancy, sexual promiscuity, and trouble with the law. According to his theory, the syndrome can lead to the rage that occasionally erupts in violent crimes committed by adoptees such as David Berkowitz, known as Son of Sam. The main popularizer of the syndrome notion is Betty Jean Lifton, an adoptee and writer for whom open adoption is an urgent cause. In *Lost & Found: The Adoption Experience*, she states: "The sad truth remains that all Adoptees have had a difficult struggle to put together an authentic self; many lead diminished or unfulfilled lives. Whether or not one wants to use the word *syndrome*, the dilemma of being adopted touches everyone. As Kirschner points out, only by facing the realities and the risks do we have a chance of preventing the syndrome from developing, and of effectively treating it when it occurs."

Acceptance or rejection of the concept of the adopted-child

syndrome dramatically divides the adoption world and splits even advocates of open adoption. A syndrome is a serious matter of mental health, critics of the notion say, and studies that seem to support the existence of this new one don't account for other possible causes of extreme behavior, such as child abuse or moves to and from unsatisfactory foster homes before adoption. Studies on which the syndrome is based have rarely distinguished between those adopted in early infancy and those adopted later, who are more likely to suffer such trauma. Critics of the syndrome see it as a theatrical and irresponsible notion that sacrifices a balanced portrait of most adoptees by using the problems of a small group to promote open adoption.

The defects in the syndrome studies are similar to those in adoption research in general, according to a wide range of adoption experts. Because adoption records remain for the most part closed (only three states maintain public adoption records; four more are now considering the policy), no one knows precisely how many adoptees there are in the United States. It is impossible for a researcher to take a true random sample as a control for a study of adoptees. The main adoption studies come out of mental-health clinics and reflect the groups in clinics rather than the wider population: for a variety of reasons, adoptive parents turn to such services more readily than other parents, and the problems of at least some of the young adoptees in clinics which are attributed to adoption almost certainly have other causes as well.

To avoid these logical pitfalls, researchers are now focusing on adoptees outside clinics. According to Ravenscroft, adoptees outside clinics tend to score lower in academic achievement and social skills than do non-adoptees and to suffer more from behavioral problems. One researcher found that some adopted women, perhaps as a result of not knowing about their own birth, experienced a slowdown in labor during their first childbirth. Another learned that almost all adopted women who have considered searching or have searched for their birth mother fantasize about what their birth mother is like and, less often, about why they were given up. As part of a quest, it seems, some young single adopted women become pregnant four and five times.

Enough adoptees, men and women, have suffered from similar problems of confusion about their identities that H. J. Sants has labeled the phenomenon "genealogical bewilderment." It is defined as a state in which adoptees have an identity shaped by what they look like, the family and circumstances they grow up in, and what they accomplish, and yet wonder who their birth parents are and what their life would have been with them.

Joyce Maguire Pavao, who directs a team of adoption counselors at the Family Center in Somerville, Massachusetts, and who is an adoptee, argues that adoptees face unusual challenges in development that are often misdiagnosed as problems. Grasping the meaning of being adopted, grieving for the loss of a life in a biological family, shaping an identity while reckoning with the added dimension of genealogical bewilderment—these tasks account for the extra psychological work that adoptees have to do. The challenges are evident in offhand circumstances. Daydreaming is part of this effort, Pavao observes, although it is often misunderstood in adoptees as an illness called attention-deficit disorder and mistreated with drugs. In her view, theories of personality development should be reorganized in terms of normal, adoption normal, and abnormal.

An essential question for adoptees is: Where do I belong? Some feel that they do not belong anywhere, or that they belong somewhere else. More than a few young adoptees believe that they come from outer space, not having been born to their adoptive mothers. But even if the question is understood to be double-edged—one goal of human development, after all, is self-possession—adoptees not uncommonly feel set apart. Frustrated at not knowing their biological roots and at being the only American adults who are prevented by law from being given information that is literally the birthright of others, some adoptees feel enslaved by a perverse system and treated like children long after they become adults. Adopted children sometimes ask, "How much did I cost?"

In conventional adoptions, adoptees sometimes blame their adoptive parents for withholding information that those parents don't have. Adoptive parents criticize themselves for not being able to prevent crises in their children which are caused by things that are out of their control. After surrendering a child, and feeling that it is wrong to talk about the loss, birth parents find themselves in the same limbo state as the children they have placed for adoption—as Leston Havens, a psychiatrist at the Harvard Medical School, recently put it at an adoption-reform conference, "unable to announce themselves to the world in the fullest sense." Some birth mothers (in one study, thirty-eight percent) who trusted the word of social workers that they would forget about their baby never did and have failed to get pregnant again. Some describe the loss of their child as an amputation. Some adoptive parents, who were led to believe that their family lives would be no different from any other, pull back in anger when their children act out and push them away. Some adoptees, bearing the Achilles' heel of their own relinquishment, have an especially hard time dealing with intimacy, separation, and loss.

Open adoption is now seen by its supporters as a way to ease these troubles. Most of the evidence about its success during the past decade is lore passed along the grapevine of supporters. In the best circumstances, birth and adoptive parents feel a measure of control they would not have otherwise, reports Sharon Kaplan, the proponent of the form of open adoption known as cooperative adoption. Adoptees treat their adoption as "a big ho-hum." In cooperative adoption, birth parents occasionally baby-sit for their birth children, and birth and adoptive parents sometimes go camping together. In open adoption, when adoptive children are asked to draw their family tree in school, they draw an orchard. Kathleen Silber, the co-author (with Phylis Speedlin) of the book *Dear Birthmother*, reports that adoptive parents who meet the birth mothers of their children feel as if "they have finally been given permission to be the parents and that they actually bond quicker with the baby, having met the birth mother."

Adults involved in the most open adoptions have invented rituals to celebrate the events. The birth and adoptive mothers shop together for the outfit the baby will wear home from the hospital. Adoptive families have welcoming ceremonies for their children in which the birth parents take part. The birth and adoptive mothers each wear a half of a necklace spelling the baby's name. Who picks the name is a major issue. For adoptive parents, choosing a name is part of "claiming behavior," Kaplan says, but it is also a right of birth parents. Sometimes birth parents choose one name and the adoptive parents another, or the birth parents give a child's christening name and the adoptive parents his daily name. One birth mother made up a name from pieces of each of the four parents' names.

For all the newness of these facts, some nineteen-fifties studies about adoptions of older children provide long-standing support for open adoption. They, too, found that the adoptions were improved by a child's continued involvement with his biological family. One study concluded: "His keeping in touch with his relatives often strengthens adoptive relationships; the child knows his adoptive parents not only accept him, but that which belongs to him." The benefits to older children, the argument now goes, apply as well to children adopted as infants. The most widespread practice of open adoption may be in American black communities, where there is a long tradition of informal adoption of children by relatives.

Perhaps the most startling claim for open adoption is not so much stories or studies as history. In a 1989 essay on open adoption, Annette Baran and Reuben Pannor contend: "There was no thought of secrecy or anonymity during the first two centuries of adoption in the United States." The colonies imported English orphans for farm labor and they were adopted by communities as apprentices and members of extended families. When an unwed woman became pregnant, she would find a family to take care of her during the pregnancy who might give the unborn child a home. The birth mother and the prospective adopters got to know and accept each other. If the couple adopted the baby, they alone raised him, "but, emotionally, there was room for the birth parent." Frequently, the birth mother's own extended family took her in and "decided which relative would adopt the child." Often, all relationships were open. In the late nineteenth century, newspapers routinely reported the details of adoption proceedings. Adoptees could obtain their original birth certificates; early adoption laws included no provisions about confidentiality. When states began to draw the veil of confidentiality over adoptions in the nineteen-twenties, they were turning from the path of open adoption followed by the country in its earliest days.

A Dangerous Mutation

"The greatest foe of open adoption today," according to one advocate of open adoption, is William Pierce, a former senior staff member of the Child Welfare League of America who is now the president of the National Committee For Adoption. Pierce describes open adoption as "very dangerous, tragic, and disastrous," and since 1980 he has been a tenacious critic of the practice. In Pierce's eyes, the history of American adoption is a morality tale whose darkest hour is open adoption. "The United States was a polyglot nation of poor immigrants with few illusions about their roots," he says. "Adoption bloomed in the American environment." According to Pierce, American law embraced the progressive purpose of protecting the best interests of adopted children: it gave them new birth certificates as a foundation for a life without the taint of illegitimacy. In the nineteen-twenties and thirties, when infertility was seen as a curse of God and involvement in a birth out of wedlock marked adults as disreputable and children as "bad seeds," confidentiality laws gave all the parties to adoptions a new beginning.

As Pierce sees it, the benefits of the law were enhanced by good works. A New York pharmaceutical manufacturer named Charles Crittenton, for example, had a sense of mission about service to women in peril, and, in 1883, founded the first of a series of Crittenton maternity homes. They helped young birth mothers place their babies and learn how to pursue useful lives. The maternity homes taught young women how to be self-sacrificing, Pierce believes, and the homes became key to American adoption. To him, a turning point came in 1954, when *Brown* v. *Board of Education*, the landmark school-desegregation case, led to calls for the desegregation of the homes as well and they "died out because they couldn't accommodate integration." (In 1966, there were 201 maternity homes in this country; by 1981, the number had dropped to ninety-nine.) Adoption agencies took their place and, as they became "professionalized" and social workers felt it a duty to ask whether pregnant young women were sure they wanted to place their babies, "the unintended consequence was that adoption was less often considered an option."

The new skepticism among potential birth mothers about adoption was reinforced by other circumstances. In the fifties and sixties, the Catholic Charities had trouble finding enough couples to adopt the babies who were available for placement. Non-Christians usually couldn't adopt through these agencies, for a dozen states had laws requiring agencies to place babies with parents whose religion was that which the birth mothers, who were often Catholic, chose on behalf of their biological children. Jewish couples therefore turned to lawyers for help with independent adoptions. Black-market baby-selling gave independent adoptions a bad name, but in 1955, when Senator Estes Kefauver, Democrat of Tennessee, wanted to outlaw them, Senator Jacob Javits, Republican of New York, "stopped him," according to Pierce, "by saying, 'My constituents won't be able to adopt.'" Eventually, after the birth-control pill, the legalization of abortion, and the rise of feminism reduced the number of babies for adoption, the success of lawyers in the field who offered some contact between birth mothers and adoptive parents forced agencies to change their ways.

The official position of Pierce on behalf of the National Committee For Adoption is that open adoption is "an untried, untested mutation of an institution that has worked for large numbers of people for decades." To Pierce, the advocates for open adoption "may be guilty of malpractice" by claiming that "confidential adoption is pathological" and that it "has created a large class of children and adults who are emotionally ill, or at least quite confused." In support of this view, some studies conclude that adoptees are "significantly more confident and view others more positively than their non-adopted peers," and that being adopted doesn't necessarily lead to "heightened stress" in adolescence. Pierce offers a list of accomplished adopted Americans (former President Gerald Ford; Dave Thomas, the founder of the Wendy's fast-food chain; Olympic medal winners Greg Louganis, the diver; Scott Hamilton, the skater; and Peter and Kitty Carruthers, pair skaters) to support the slogan "Adopted kids have great expectations." In a textbook titled *Child Welfare Services*, Alfred Kadushin, professor emeritus of social work at the University of Wisconsin at Madison, and Judith A. Martin, associate professor of social work at the University of Pittsburgh, provide a review of adoption studies. Their summary generally supports Pierce. Two of every three adoptions were judged "unequivocally successful"; more than four out of five were in the acceptable or successful range; and fewer than one out of five were "failures." (The failure rate for independent adoptions, twenty-five percent, seems to be higher than for agency adoptions, fifteen percent, according to Kadushin and Martin.) While the number of adopted children at mental-health clinics is disproportionately high, Kadushin and Martin comment, it "may be lower than that which we have a right to expect, given the insults to psychic health that many adopted children have endured." In any case, adult adoptees use psychiatric facilities no more, proportionately, than do non-adoptees.

Where the advocates of open adoption find value, Pierce sees risk. For birth mothers, Pierce contends, the message of open adoption is that you can give up your child without needing to separate from him, and "have it both ways." To Pierce, the message is an illusion with sad consequences. Birth mothers don't view their child as lost, don't mourn the loss, and, however positive the recognition they enjoy for their instrumental role in the adoption, they fail to move on with their lives. The risk to adoptive parents is that their relationship to the birth mother will jeopardize their bond with the child, making them feel shame about their infertility and guilt about taking the child, and as if they are caretakers standing in for the birth mother. Continued association with the birth mother can make them feel concerned about whether she approves of how they are bringing up the baby. A bad impression of the birth mother can infect their views of the child. As for an adopted child, contact with his birth mother can backfire, inflating his sense of rejection by her and raising anxieties about her taking him back or about his adoptive parents abandoning him, too.

Studies by a team of social workers with St. Mary's Services, an Episcopal child-welfare agency in Chicago, support these contentions. They found that, for birth mothers, open adoption is a complex, sometimes deceptive choice leading to a relationship for which there is no social precedent. Sometimes a young birth mother looks for a new set of parents in the adoptive parents. Often she expects to have a role in the family, like an aunt, a baby-sitter, a sister, or a godmother, and doesn't face the fact that she has given up the child. For adoptive parents, open adoption can hinder "any healthy parent's capacity to form a secure and comfortably close bond with an infant." The team concluded that advocates of open adoption often given "the clear message" not only that adoptive parents "owe something to the birth parents but also that they are not full-fledged parents" and that it is proper for them to give up their rights to privacy in exchange for the chance to adopt a child. As for an adopted child, there are risks of "serious interference" at every stage of his development. An open adoption is likely to leave him feeling more like a foster child, lacking a sense of permanence within his adoptive family, and to force him to reckon with his adopted status abruptly and prematurely, when it is best for him to assimilate this fact gradually over time.

When Bill Pierce appears on TV shows to talk about adoption, he is by turns sober, fractious, and self-righteous. His style can rankle even those who agree with him, and who sometimes wish that an advocate with a less insistent way of promoting conventional adoption occasionally drew the spotlight. Pierce specializes in the attention-grabbing analogy, comparing the purchase of black-market babies with buying cocaine, and claiming that it is easier to get a child through an independent adoption than to get a dog from the pound. He is a skillful exploiter of sensationalism. On the TV show *Geraldo*, he appeared with a young single mother who was bringing up her baby but had been lured by a newspaper ad to Louisiana, where a man offered her a lot of money for the baby and any others she would produce for him. Pierce came close to suggesting that the young woman's experience was typical and that all intermediaries involved in independent adoptions were, as he put it, "procurers."

As Pierce often suggests, the term "open" currently wears a white hat and steers a team of horses named honesty, tolerance, acceptance, and fairness. The term "closed," which is used by open-adoption advocates in place of "conventional" or "confidential," wears an eye patch and a leer and follows a set of mules named secrecy, narrow-mindedness, punishment, and prejudice. It is a particular frustration for Pierce that the concept of openness in adoption is so loose. In his view, open adoption was well defined by Annette Baran and her colleagues when they proposed that its core is identifying information, which means that the birth and adoptive parents know one another's names and where to find one another. The absolute confidentiality that he believes made American adoptions successful for generations is in jeopardy.

Pierce resents the elasticity of the "openness" concept because he thinks that it misappropriates, to the credit of open adoption, changes that have taken place during the past fifteen years in conventional adoption. On this point, Pierce enjoys wide support among believers in conventional adoption. The team from St. Mary's Services noted: "To our knowledge, secret or closed adoptions, where no information is provided to birth parents and adoptive parents about the other, has not been part of good agency practice for years. In conventional adoptions, all nonidentifying and medical data regarding the parents is exchanged between adoptive and biological parents through the agency." Birth mothers play a role in picking the kind of family they want their children to go to, if not in the specific final selection, which, according to the St. Mary's team, is best made by trained professionals. Conventional agencies discourage contact between birth mothers and their babies after placement, until the child turns eighteen, and both express a wish to meet, but they encourage adopted children to visit the agency, to talk with birth mothers other than their own and learn why they are planning to give up their babies. Conventional agencies sympathetically counsel birth and adoptive parents about each other's fear, hope, pain, and perspective.

If the extremes in adoption are absolute confidentiality and the exchange of identifying information (cooperative adoption being a rare form), the evolution in conventional adoption has not yet taken it as far as the middle ground. While some agencies that belong to the National Committee For Adoption have quietly broken ranks with Pierce on this issue, he disapproves of many of the steps of what is sometimes called semi-open adoption: "an exchange of nonidentifying information, pictures, letters, gifts, and possibly one face-to-face meeting involving no exchange of identities," according to a consensus definition written by Ruth G. McRoy, a professor of social work, Harold Grotevant, a professor of child development, and Kerry White, a researcher in child development, at the University of Texas. Pierce discourages as a form of coercion one-time face-to-face meetings between potential birth mothers and prospective adopters. He thinks the harm that could result from their exchanging letters outweighs the prospects for good. ("A very fine birth mother with poor penmanship might be judged harshly and unfairly as being 'sloppy' or 'stupid' by the adoptive parents or others.") The same goes for gifts. He asks: What if a family has two adoptive children, and the birth mother of one sends "a hand-knitted baby cap" while the other sends "a diamond-studded cross that's a family heirloom"? Won't the gifts make the children feel unequal?

Pierce says that open adoption is like the synthetic hormone DES, which was used to keep pregnant women from miscarrying but resulted in difficulty for their daughters in carrying fetuses to term: the people who invented it may have had good intentions, but the result will be widespread suffering in the years ahead. Although he makes a point of separating open adoption from all others, he treats most practices of openness as steps on a slippery slope. Since in his opinion open adoption is so risky, he spends a lot of energy to keep it from ever happening. He tries to prevent birth mothers from being "defrauded" out of their babies by middlemen who make promises of continuing involvement that can't be kept. ("In open adoption, the mother makes her own decision about who adopts her baby," says one agency's ad, in which a photo shows the birth mother seated in a wing chair holding the baby, the birth father kneeling next to the chair, and the adoptive parents with their arms around each other standing behind. "You can choose who you feel will make the best parents to raise your child.") He tries to protect prospective adopters from being pressured into a meeting with potential birth parents, because they fear that otherwise they won't be selected to raise the child. (" 'Open Adoption' is 'Emotional Blackmail,' " declared a headline of the National Committee For Adoption's bimonthly newsletter.)

The originators of the concept of open adoption, Annette

Baran and Reuben Pannor, also protest the way in which some lawyers and new adoption agencies use open adoption as a marketing tool. "When we developed the concept, we were very idealistic about it," Baran said recently. "What's happened is that the entrepreneurs, motivated by profit, have insinuated themselves into the open-adoption system. They are empathetic, but into business. The opportunists are leaving us idealists gasping for breath."

The fact that Pierce, on the one hand, and Baran and Pannor, on the other, disapprove of commerce in adoption doesn't mean they have come around to the same point of view. They still see themselves as guardians of different interests. Although each side presents its approach as the honorable way to serve all three of the main parties to an adoption, each also acknowledges that the parties sometimes have conflicting interests: what is right for a birth mother may be wrong for the child, the St. Mary's Services team observed, and what makes sense for the adoptive parents may not for the birth mother. From the start, the open adoption envisioned by Baran and Pannor was shaped by, and has come back to embrace, the cause of the birth mother. The conventional adoption that Pierce defends appears frequently to focus on the needs of the adopted child, but its claims about how to satisfy those needs often favor the adoptive parents as well. The irreconcilable difference between traditional adoption (the term Pierce favors) and open adoption, as he sees it, is the sense of entitlement to be a full and independent adoptive parent versus the inevitable sharing of that responsibility with the birth mother: for the adoptee, one leads to clarity and the other to confusion about who his "real" parents are.

The alignments of open adoption and birth mothers, on the one hand, and conventional adoption and adoptive parents, on the other, can be explained by a basic, if knotty, disagreement about human capacity. Open adoption depends on the optimistic notion that people can handle unfamiliar, even unprecedented, relationships. But, for all its optimism, the concept is also based on the premise that any adoption is second-best—that a child should be with his biological parents if possible, and if not, that his life with his adoptive family shouldn't cut him off from his biological roots. The optimism about human potential is overtaken by the negative notion at the source of open adoption.

The National Committee For Adoption turns these views upside down. It is not sanguine about the human potential to adapt to open adoption, and sees no need to try. On the other hand, it sees no end to the mixture of forces that cause some babies to be available for adoption and some adults to want to adopt them. Pierce and many others believe that, by and large, the American adoption experience has been excellent. An ad for the Committee, showing a picture of a healthy white infant and written from the point of view of a birth mother, declares: "I Know My Baby Will Be Part of a Loving Family Because I'm Choosing Adoption."

At a 1989 adoption-reform meeting, Reuben Pannor complained about the transformation of adoption from a means of finding homes for homeless children into a way to provide children for childless couples. He described the adoption world as a domain of heartache, and citing the model of Australia, where the government vigorously teaches family planning and infant adoptions have dwindled to a low number, he proclaimed his hope that infant adoptions will die out in the United States and become a footnote to the history of American child welfare. If childless couples want to be parents, he advised, they have no *right* to adopt healthy infants; they can always care for some of the thousands of older, handicapped, or needy children in foster care.

The wide differences between how each school views adoption and the complexities of each individual adoption, if only in terms of the number of people involved and the divergence of their interests, mean that neither school is likely to be wholly satisfied by any one study purporting to make a comprehensive judgment about open adoption. But advocates for both open and conventional adoption cite the same ongoing work, by Ruth G. McRoy and her colleagues at the University of Texas, as the most promising research about it.

In 1988, McRoy and her colleagues brought out a monograph called *Openness in Adoption* in which they presented findings from a pilot study of seventeen adoptive families and the birth parents. "Given the balance of the risks and values of openness in adoption, the greatest benefit and the least risk seem to occur in families with semi-open adoptions," they concluded.

According to the McRoy group, the birth parents in a semi-open adoption can have the "security of knowing" about the child, and may receive occasional pictures and updated reports. The adoptive families are likely to be more stable without the involvement of the birth parents; the adoptive parents "can avoid the interference of regular contact" with them, but know that the birth parents are "easily accessible" for any information that might be needed to "help the child understand the adoption." The adoptees have more information than they would in a conventional adoption and can "develop a more positive sense of self" as a result. But they "are not subjected to the possible confusion of roles among adoptive parents and birth parents that may occur in open adoptions." By the Baran–Pannor definition of open adoption, which is also Pierce's, the Texas group stopped short of endorsing that concept, but the researchers lean toward the open camp. "Some families who begin with a semi-open adoption may later choose to increase the degree of contact with birth parents," they observed. They also cautioned: "Fully disclosed openness, while it has worked very well for some families . . . presents many unanticipated challenges to all members of the adoption triad. The decision to move to fully disclosed openness should not be made lightly."

The Aftermath

During the months after Rebecca's birth, Peggy refined her understanding of open adoption to a parable: Rebecca had come to Peggy as a little soul, and she had found the baby's true parents. Everything had gone perfectly; Peggy said she felt that someone was watching out for everyone involved; and her only disappointment about her experience, she said emphatically, was that she couldn't go on TV and give lectures about the benefits of adoption generally, since she didn't want to reveal her secret to her parents. She and Tom displayed a casual attitude even when they discussed big questions about Rebecca's adoption, like their views about Rebecca's religion: they didn't care what faith she was brought up in as long as she was loved, they said, and, while Lee was a Protestant and Dan was a nominal but essentially secular Jew, his doting on Rebecca ordained that she was going to be a Jewish American Princess.

In September, Peggy and Tom went to a Renaissance Fair. Peggy saw a booth with a tarot-card reader and said, "Let's have a hoot . . . I sit down and ask a very innocent question, like 'What's the best time of the year to get married?' And she lays out all these fertility cards, and she's, like, 'This is not the question that you wanted. This is another question and I'm going to ask it: Did you recently lose a child and are you planning to remarry?' And the woman was telling me, 'There's going to be some pain.' " Pain was a constant for Peggy and Tom, binding them together with their secret but also pushing them apart. Tom worried that they were going "to let the cat out of the bag," and Peggy, having lived without Tom for two months, considered whether she should try the same thing back home, where she was again staying with her parents. Peggy and Tom talked about Rebecca a lot: they guessed that Dan, for all his liberal ideas, would be conservative and a disciplinarian when it came to his daughter, because he was so smitten by her; and that Lee, though she loved Rebecca as much as Dan did, was likely to be the "better 'parent.' " They comforted themselves with the idea that if anything happened to Lee and Dan, Rebecca would come back to them. Peggy and Tom were mistaken, for, once the adoption was approved by a judge, they would have no legal tie to her.

A letter from Peggy to the Stones, September 13, 1988: "I've decided to quit my job, drop out of society, and wear live animal hats. Not really. So what's new with you? I miss you all so much—please let me come up and do it again, well, at least visit." She chatted about losing weight (on "the Amazing Birth Mother Diet"), and some hot tank tops her mother had bought for her. ("I look like an individual from the Combat Zone when she helps pick out my clothes," she wrote, referring to Boston's red-light district. "Even Daddy's saying, 'Hubba, hubba.' Please, Dan, don't say that to Rebecca.") She closed: "Tom and I just wanted to let you all know we are thinking about you, and loving having brought Rebecca into this world. I mean it when I say I would do it again for you. You are all in our prayers. We love you."

September 27, 1988: "Dear Otis, So how's tricks? Aughh —are Lee & Dan reading this, too??? Oh, well, tell them I miss them frightfully, I'm sitting here reading my psychology assignment on fear. Did you know I'm anal retentive? How gross can you be—oh, please, don't scare me, I'm Jung and easily Freudened (a bad joke that my psychotic teacher cackled over for ages) . . .

"Tom still has not bought me an engagement ring, not that it matters. I still love him but I've decided to Hell with a customized Dragon interlocking wedding band. I want a DIA-MOND and a gold band from Sears. Bland but functional. Also, I want to postpone the wedding until July 20th, our third anniversary, so we can save up enough to put a down payment down on a house . . .

"I realized this summer on one of my overdue days as Re-becca galloped about my uterus that I needed to just be me. As in a singular individual, not two people in one body, or even two people united in pregnancy, just me. Some nights I miss pregnancy so much, and I miss Boston horribly. I hope being parents is better than you thought. Tom and I are jealous of you all, because you get to see every clever thing that little one does. Tom and I both feel very good about her, we know she'll be wonderful. I miss her little kicks and nudges, all the stuff that was bad or scary has faded like a mist. It's all there but it doesn't seem as important as having brought a little angel into the world. Despite all this sentimentality let me be frank. I love not being MATERNAL, I'm wearing tight jeans and tank tops everywhere . . ."

October 3, 1988: "Tom is leaving his job, which is putting a lot of pressure on us. I decided it would be best to postpone the engagement until he is settled career-wise a little bit. This summer taught me a great deal about security—I really need it and I am just a little bit too fragile still to cope with extra stress and tension. So we decided, to keep families happy and credit/bank people paid, we should wait until Tom has a def-inite positive cash flow to announce the impending nuptials.

"We are rather yuppie-like. We were talking about investing in a CD or mutual fund, I am too business-oriented. Most girls my age daydream about either little houses or a career. Since I already have a family (Rebecca, I count her even though she is there) I really want a career for a while before I become a super Good Housekeeping kind of person . . .

"I love Tom beyond everything, he still feels terrible about the pain I went through. He is wonderful to me, and he is so baby-oriented now. Rebecca is a reason that Tom is unhappy with his job—he realized that if he could create life and achieve what he did this summer, he wants a job he feels productive and successful in. I'd really like to come up around my 21st birthday, since Rebecca will be 4 months by then, and that is a great age, and she'll be talking and working on her thesis paper on the theories of gravitational polarity so maybe she can schedule me in for a few snuggles."

Dan couldn't get enough of Rebecca: her little "maaas" that sounded like a goat's bleating; her alertness; her tiny hands. Cradling Rebecca on his shoulder, he recounted the story of her adoption as if it were a rare adventure. He acknowledged that he was proud of things about Rebecca he had nothing to do with, like her size at birth (eight pounds, twenty-one inches), which to him promised a striking height. Lee turned out to be less ready for her. She felt a lingering sadness about her infertility—she had miscarried three times in three years, and it appeared that she could not sustain a pregnancy—and felt reverberations from the August weekend when her fear that she might lose Rebecca gave her the sense that she was having another miscarriage. About a month after Rebecca was born, Lee and her friend Miriam Cato were out pushing the baby in a stroller and Lee was talking about Peggy. Several times, she called her Rebecca's mother. Miriam had liked Peggy ("She's *definitely* not from earth," Miriam decided. "She's too spiritual"), but finally she interrupted to say, "You are Rebecca's mom. I don't want to talk about Peggy all the time. I just want this to be you, me, and Rebecca."

Peggy's letters made Lee feel even more vulnerable. When the third one arrived, Lee took it to a dinner with the Roses and read it aloud. The letter set off an evening of talk about whether they should be truly worried how Peggy was doing. The talk carried over for weeks afterward. To Dan, the letters said that Peggy had finally opened the lid on feelings she had suppressed during the summer in order to carry out her adoption plan. To the Roses, they were reminders of how precarious the adoption had seemed at moments in August, and why they would not choose an open adoption for themselves. "The thing that scares me about it is the risk that you get emotionally committed to a child who isn't even born yet, and that carries with it the risk that you will suffer a terrible loss if the adoption doesn't go through," Jim explained. "The second concern is that you will be in a permanent three-way relationship with someone who you haven't really chosen. It's very risky. It could be absolutely wonderful; it could be terrible. There's no way of knowing."

In confident moments, Dan felt that he had experienced nothing to undermine his faith in open adoption. "If I were adopted, I am certain that I would want to know my birth parents," he said in October. "I just can't imagine not." The birth parents were the missing piece of a puzzle. He retained "enormous respect and affection" for Peggy, and it seemed wonderful to him that eventually Rebecca could experience that too. "It's not a little thing, where one comes from," he said. Dan also kept imagining himself a birth parent. He and Lee made two sets of albums telling Rebecca's story, one with pictures of her birth, the other without. When he saw himself in a picture, he felt lucky, excited, grateful. On the other hand, he said, "When I look at a picture I'm not in, I identify with the birth mother and think that we wanted something so badly that we couldn't do for ourselves." As he looked at pictures of Rebecca and Peggy together, the concept of adoption struck him as base and acquisitive. "Choosing to adopt doesn't feel noble," he said one day. "It feels pathetic."

The cure for Dan and Lee's discomfort was to hope for the best for Peggy. It concerned them that she seemed to have isolated herself from anyone who could get under her shell of self-control, and they were glad when she started phoning just to chat. The calls came every ten days or so, at three or four in the afternoon. The talk was about Peggy and Tom, or tax forms Peggy had to fill out, or nothing much—less about Rebecca than they had expected it would be. The Stones began sending packets of photographs of Rebecca to Peggy and Tom, who said they loved them. The Stones' relationship with Peggy and Tom mystified some of their friends who knew about it. Miriam Cato said, "I don't know what birth mother wants to see fifty pictures of the baby, no matter how wonderful the thing is. Why would Lee want to send pictures, unless Peggy asked?" In October, Lee's mind-body group (the group of infertile women with whom she had learned to meditate) gave her a baby shower. "A lot of people in my group were unbelievably upset by the Rebecca story," Lee said. "They couldn't believe how close we were to the birth mother. It was threatening to them. They worried that the birth mother would haunt us. They thought Dan and I were in over our heads."

In early November, Peggy sent an upbeat letter. ("I may have an opportunity to begin a management trainee job [$24,000 per year?!!] full-time after exams. I would have to take night classes to finish college, so it would probably take until '90 to graduate, but I'd be able to move out and live on my own, with my dog, of course.") Every once in a while, Peggy felt she got pushed backward: she had used her parents' address on her Boston hospital records, marking them "strictly confidential," and in the winter she got a letter asking if she wanted her daughter to take part in an eye test sponsored by the hospital. ("I killed that real fast," Tom said.) Peggy sometimes felt that she was enduring a trial. She became intolerant of her friends' problems ("They think it's a tragedy when they get home from the beauty parlor and their perm hasn't taken"), and occasionally, in her view, too blunt ("I've gotten rid of a lot of leechy friends").

But by January, when she sent the Stones some Christmas gifts and told them about finding a townhouse to move into with a couple of roommates, she said she had her momentum back. She was working full-time for a clothing store as a salesperson, she reported, and said she was finishing up her college work through independent studies. She was about to start "Catholic lessons," she said, so she could convert before Tom and she got married.

By January, Lee's feelings for Rebecca matched Dan's, and they found that they had become an informal adoption-counseling service—advising people who called them how to move beyond infertility to thinking about adoption, whether to adopt, how to adopt. A friend's sister in West Virginia knew of a twenty-year-old pharmacology student due in April who was looking for a couple to adopt her baby, and called them. Some Jewish friends knew of an evangelical Christian birth mother in a commune outside Las Vegas, and asked their help in wrestling with the question of how the baby she was carrying, not born of a Jewish mother, would fit into their Jewish family.

A couple of times, Peggy arranged and then postponed a visit to the Stones. Each revised date for the visit was close enough to seem plausible but far enough away to stay out of clear focus. Lee and Dan began to feel as if they had lost touch with her. In mid-February, almost six months after Rebecca's birth, Peggy called and said, "Could you see if Colleen will be around for when we come up, which we're thinking of doing soon?" It was Peggy's way of saying she was coming, and her indirectness threw Lee; it brought back the fear of losing Rebecca. Lee wondered if some of their friends were right that nothing good could come of further contact with Peggy. Dan, on the other hand, said that they had always trusted Peggy and that there was no reason to stop. Every time their adoption entered a new stage, the fears that others had about it were alleviated by the nature of the relationship that he and Lee had with Peggy. For lack of a better term to define their complicated ties to one another, Dan proposed that Rebecca's birth and adoptive parents think of themselves as *machetunim*, an all-purpose Yiddish word describing intricate relationships by marriage or in extended families. By the week before the visit, Lee was excited, too.

That week, Peggy and Tom were run down from work, nervous about the trip, and beleaguered by little details, like trying to buy Rebecca a pair of pint-sized Vuarnet sunglasses. They described themselves as an old married couple who never went to the clubs anymore: they just worked, got together at one of their places, ate poorly, and went to sleep. Each place was somehow barren: Peggy's townhouse was sparsely decorated with second-hand furniture, and the refrigerator was almost empty; Tom's apartment, while packed with well-tended hi-fi equipment, was a mess of submarine-sandwich wrappers and other fast-food debris. Peggy was fidgety about missing a rent payment. Even to Tom, her story about the rent was vague, but she said she had put her roommates' rent money into her bank account, had lost a credit card, and, after the bank froze her account when she reported the card missing, found herself unable to write a check to cover the rent. Tom figured that Peggy would solve the problem. His mind was on Boston.

"One part just wants to be strong again and uninvolved, and the other has to be there, has to see her," Tom said. About Rebecca, they had questions (Were they like Rebecca's godparents?), speculations ("My body, Peggy's personality," Tom said), and stray thoughts (Peggy: "Sometimes I think, Oh, my God, I'm going to have a twelve-year-old daughter in the year 2000"). Their thoughts about Lee and Dan led back to Rebecca. Tom remarked one day, "Dan says she's a gift from God. As a couple, they're so strong. Rebecca's either going to be an incredible egomaniac, tempered by Lee's sweetness, or I don't know what." Peggy responded, "I don't think she'll be modest." They arranged to stay with the Roses on their visit and decided that if they had to cut the visit short they would. After looking into buses and flights to Boston, they compromised on a train from Wilmington that would get them in early in the morning.

Reunion

On Saturday, March 18, Lee woke up, restless, at 5:30 a.m., as if she were going on a trip. Dan got up half an hour later and tried to get rid of his nervousness by stretching. Lee gave Rebecca a chamomile bath and dressed her in purple pants, a yellow shirt, shoes and socks, and a green jester's hat with stars on it. At 8:05, Peggy and Tom stepped off the train at South Station ("I was, like, chewing my fingernails, saying, 'This meeting has to be so careful, to set the tone,' " Peggy said later) and the Stones weren't there. As Tom was dialing their number, Dan strolled into the station. Lee hadn't wanted Dan to see Peggy and Tom before she did, so the Stones had been in their car in the taxi line out front, hoping that Peggy and Tom would find them.

"Peggy is wearing her white Japanese baseball jacket, and everything is really familiar," Dan recalled later. "They seem surprisingly refreshed for people who took an all-night train ride. I'm so used to carrying Peggy's bag that I pick it up, and we joke about that. We go outside and Lee is beaming and so happy. Rebecca is asleep in the back seat."

Dan was putting the bags in the car as Peggy and Tom got their first look at Rebecca, now almost seven months old.

Through the rear window, he followed the scene: Peggy sliding in and staring at the baby for the first time since August; Rebecca sleepily opening her eyes; Tom staring at Rebecca, too. Peggy thought, she said later, Oh, God, she looks great. Tom thought: She has big, sad eyes, just like Peggy. They drove to the Roses', to see Dina, Jim, and Jacob, and found everything friendly and disorganized. "Lee and Dan are so into Rebecca, but she couldn't crawl yet, so she sort of lay on the ground and paddled," Peggy said. "We handed her back and forth." When Tom held the baby, she cried. ("You know when you're on a plane that's gonna go down," he said.) When Rebecca cried with Peggy, too, Dan realized she acted the way she did when she was held by someone she didn't know.

After a while, Peggy and Tom tried to nap. That didn't work, so the whole group took off on errands. They stopped to see a condominium that Dan and Lee had just bought, which was in the middle of renovations. Peggy and Tom lingered in the room that was going to be Rebecca's. Dan heard them say how great it would be for her when she was a teenager: "I had an ear out: Would they claim her? But they just didn't do it. They seemed concerned about Rebecca at every level. We did a lot of passing Rebecca around, me to Lee to Peggy, especially. At one point, I was changing Rebecca and Tom left the room and Peggy watched. It was the first chance she'd had to see Rebecca's little body—and how could she not think of her own body and its relation to Rebecca's? But she was just attentive to Rebecca, and that was that." After a lunch out, Tom and Peggy went back to the Roses' house, and Jim and Dina suggested that they try another nap. They lay awake talking about how wonderful Rebecca was: how she smelled, what her skin looked like, whether her not crawling yet meant there was something wrong with her, or that she was so smart she was waiting until she could stand up and walk.

At the Stones' old place, where Dan and Lee had returned with Rebecca so the baby could sleep, Rebecca woke up in a happy mood and Lee and Dan called Peggy and Tom to say they thought it would be a nice time for them to play with her. By the time they got there with the Roses a couple of hours later, Rebecca had gone back to sleep, but she woke up for an encore. Lee gave Peggy and Tom some packs of fresh pictures of Rebecca, which they joked about trading like base-ball cards, and showed them some other things.

When Colleen Rule arrived, the core of the summer group was reconstituted—Peggy, the Stones, and the Roses, as well as Tom and Colleen—and it felt like a good family reunion: funny, personal, irreverent. Tom and Peggy told stories about their friends back home ("Totally implausible and, if true, amazing stories," Jim concluded) and had the others in stitches. Peggy: "Colleen never really loses it, but she has a great belly laugh and then you *have* to tell another story, because she's laughing so hard. She kissed everybody, and everybody had these huge lipstick smears."

At the Roses', after midnight, Peggy decided that it felt good to be back in Boston, and Tom felt that his fears about how she would fare on the trip had been baseless. (Tom: "It was, like, you plan for a bad storm when you hear the weather forecast.") With the summer behind her, Peggy said that she didn't need Tom to serve as a safe haven from the pressures of Boston anymore. He could be involved. Lee and Dan sensed the same thing. "He was warm, open, and really plugged in," Lee said.

The next morning, Peggy and Tom came back for breakfast and to talk about the future. Peggy said later, "We didn't want to interfere or make them feel like nonparents—like they had to show us what great parents they are and entertain us. It was very hard to come right out and say, 'What do you want from us, in the next eighteen to twenty-one years, as far as Rebecca goes?' They told us, 'We'll just take it one day at a time.' Dan said something that really thrilled me, which was 'The more people who love Rebecca, the better, and the more people she knows who love her, the better.' We're certainly not going to be treated as fake members of the family—this

is your Aunt Peggy and Uncle Tom. Dan feels we are definitely members of their extended family, not just Rebecca's.
Lee told me a number of times that I was like her sister—
because we're almost the right ages, too, that I could have
been a younger sister. They are very interested in keeping it
very family-oriented. I suppose Rebecca, by the time she is
eighteen, will feel she has thousands of people who worship
her every step—the Rebecca Cult, all the people who wear
their hair fuzzed up and drool and suck pacifiers—which
wouldn't surprise Dan and Lee at all, if it happened—but it
was great to have Dan and Lee come right out and say, 'We
want you to stay in contact, but let's play it by ear and see
what happens.' "

On the way to the train station, Tom asked if Lee and Dan
were happy with Rebecca. Lee thought he was fishing for
compliments and teased him. Dan thought Tom was being
serious and said, "We've never been happier in our lives."
Rebecca was fussing as they reached the station, and Peggy
and Tom dashed—relieved not to have to contend with the
baby, they said not long after the visit. They were confident
that they would see the Stones soon. The only question mark
about the weekend for Lee and Dan, which they didn't raise,
was that Peggy seemed to have gained a lot of weight.

Soon after the reunion, Dan remarked, "There's something
so poignant about the whole situation. It's two young people
who are really in love with each other, and who got pregnant
by accident, and don't have the money at this point in their
lives to take care of the baby the way they want to, and it's
two older people who love each other and have the resources
and can't have a child on their own, which they desperately
want, and the exchange between them of this baby, with this
incredible well of good will and a deep affection for each other.
In my own mind, I ascribe much of this to Peggy: We all
could behave in ways that make it impossible to carry on a
relationship, but she seems to be the central figure. She's the
one who got things in motion; she picked us from Diane's list;

she phoned us; she asked Lee to be the first person to hold Rebecca; she phoned us to visit; she never makes us feel anything less than Rebecca's parents, without denying her role in the process. I don't see how she does it, how she has such a clear vision. If we felt that Peggy was covetous of Rebecca, jealous of us, deeply hurt—all of which she has a right to feel—it would make it very difficult for us to have a relationship with her. It would complicate our feelings for Rebecca. It would hurt very much to know she was feeling pain. But that doesn't happen when we're together, when we're in touch. In that sense, this is so much her creation.

"In some ways, I'm grateful, and also don't think that's the right word. Because Peggy and Tom don't present themselves that way—there's some kind of equality. The feeling that they have a place in our family is stronger than ever. I have no idea how it can be realized. It has a lot to do with them as well as us. It's something we can't know yet. I would like it that we do see each other from time to time: that Rebecca sees them and knows them and takes comfort from that. The whole thing is that I know, as I come to another plateau in this process, it will have to be reinvented in some way. That's not neat. It could backfire in some horrible way. But I can't help believing that our good feelings for them are well founded, that the lengths they've gone to assure that Rebecca has a good home with us are an expression of love."

In the days after Peggy and Tom left, Lee fantasized about attending their wedding. After Tom gave Peggy a summer of "freedom" in 1989 to make up for the one she missed the year before, he was going to announce the engagement, he said. He and Peggy had told the Stones they had "penciled in" a date in February of 1990. "If we brought Rebecca, I'm sure Peggy's mother would know the instant she saw her what was up," Lee said soon after the visit. Tom had also invited the Stones to the house his family owned at Rehoboth Beach. Lee:

"For a moment I thought, How great! We'll drive to Delaware!"

The Stones conferred with the Roses, and, in Dan's view, Dina came up with the best formulation about the heart of the matter. "Dina said it seemed clear to her that Peggy was not involved with Rebecca in a way you might fear," Dan said, "but that she'd never be far away either. Peggy doesn't act as if she has a parental claim on Rebecca, but she's not going away. Both things are very nice. That speaks to a contradiction and it seems very natural."

Jim Rose was more dubious. He couldn't imagine a weekend that could have turned out any better; he envied the Stones for knowing so much about Peggy and Tom, and about their feelings for Rebecca; and he admired Dan and Lee's faith in their ability to rise to unfamiliar challenges—they had made a specialty of it. But he also wondered how long the relationship could last, and thought the Stones were afraid of hurting Peggy and Tom—by cutting ties with them, for example, even if that seemed in Rebecca's best interests. The risks involved for everyone remained high, he felt, and the current chemistry among the four adults was no guarantee that their friendship would continue indefinitely.

"If Peggy and Tom get married, and they have good jobs and kids and things turn out well, who knows how that will affect their outlook, since they'll be in a position to give Rebecca what they didn't think they could last year," he said one day. "Or, if they split up and their jobs aren't going well, they could look to her for satisfaction. They're not going to suddenly turn into dreadful people, but who knows what will happen."

Peggy and Tom also took stock. They were grateful that they had had the chance to clear the air with the Stones about some issues, like the Jewish Family Service, which had required that she document her expenses during her pregnancy before it would reimburse her. Peggy: "We got to sit down and talk about how we both were led to believe that their main concern was somebody other than us. It just happened to be because of red tape. It wasn't because Elayna Kirschtel had decided to make my summer the worst of my entire life and create a living hell for me. She was going by a book that didn't apply to the situation; she couldn't give me answers because she didn't know them; and they weren't prepared to deal with an open adoption. We finally sat down and talked about the money thing—how frustrating it was for me to call every day and nobody called me back. Dan and Lee said it was just as frustrating for them." (The Jewish Family Service eventually reimbursed Peggy for toilet articles, some maternity clothes, transportation between Wilmington and Boston for her and Tom, meals, and miscellaneous expenses of $1,500. Adoption expenses for the Stones totaled $14,000. That figure included these expenses of Peggy's; the payment to Diane Michelsen; the Stones' trip to meet Michelsen; the trip to Washington to meet Peggy and Tom; and about $4,500 for hospital costs [Peggy's bill for anesthesia was a thousand dollars] not covered by insurance. The Stones' expenses were close to the average cost of a domestic adoption through an agency in 1989, according to the National Committee For Adoption. The Stones had not paid for Peggy's housing, which can add as much as five thousand dollars to the cost of an adoption.)

Peggy was full of advice for potential birth mothers: "For fear that you might have bad days afterward if you give this child up, don't keep this child. If you're going to keep a child to whom you're not going to be able to give what you want to give it, the pain is going to be much worse. To continually have a baby crying because you're not able to be with it, or you're working full-time and you're exhausted when you get home and can't take care of it—that's bad enough, if that's the way you planned it. But if it's unplanned and unexpected, and you really feel in your heart that maybe you should have given the baby up, there's going to be a lot more pain out of it. It's not just going to be your pain—then you've taken some-body who didn't ask for it and included him or her. I'm not going to say the pain isn't there, but it's just one of those things. Another thing birth parents have to realize is that it's a decision you live with every day. I think it differs greatly from abortion, because abortion is an ending. This is a beginning. We're looking at a whole life. As long as we're on earth, together or separately, Rebecca is always going to be a part of it. No matter what she does with her life, she's always going to be part of our life picture."

Seeing themselves as a couple, Peggy and Tom looked at their future together. Peggy said it would be hard for her "to play the 'first pregnancy' game": she had already had the initial thrill of seeing her baby on a sonogram and hearing the fetal heartbeat. Tom commented, "One thing that adoptive parents fear is their child saying 'My *real* parents wouldn't have done this to me.' Since we haven't gone through any of the sleepless nights with Rebecca or things like that, I hope I don't say, 'Our *first* child wasn't this hard.' " Both said that, instead of making it more difficult for them to put the adoption behind them, contact with the Stones provided a valuable incentive. Tom: "It makes us madder that we can't get on with our lives— that we're not moving faster."

Peggy and Tom also reconfirmed the decision not to tell their families. "They take things very personally," Peggy said. "Our families would have assumed it was something they did wrong and they should have done something to fix or prevent it. We didn't feel like having this open to a family forum of two very strong sets of parents telling me how my heart should be feeling about things and telling me what I should do— because that to me wasn't in my best interests and it wasn't in the baby's best interests to have its grandparents guiding this big decision about its life. I'd be put in a position of taking a back seat. We did what we sincerely believe was the right thing to do."

Tom: "She was in her junior year of college, I'd been recently unemployed and was employed but at a low-paying position—there was too much possibility for self-destruction here. I know that every day Peggy and I get stronger is a day closer to the time we feel it's right to tell our parents, when we've gotten past the pain and can deal with the pain it might give them." Tom again: "After we saw Dan and Lee this weekend, it became less important for me to tell our parents. First I thought—it's their grandchild. But after seeing Dan and Lee, I realized it's their *biological* grandchild. Someday, we may tell them."

Peggy: "A lot of it depends on how things go. If Rebecca wants to be part of our lives, I am not going to hide Rebecca. If she wants to visit us, or stay with us for a week, or if she wants to come down and see us for a month in the summer, when she's older—or if she wants to go to school down here; there are plenty of schools in the Delaware area, and it would be dumb not to give her that chance—she may not want to meet her biological grandparents. She might; if she does, I want to give her that opportunity, in which case I suppose we'll have to give my parents a little more warning than 'Your biological grandchild is coming.' I'm assuming Rebecca will eventually get to the point where she wants to come down and meet people. If she does, that's when I will open it up to my parents for discussion, because then it will be their decision. But until then my parents are not getting a voice in this discussion, because my parents can be very irrational." As for not revealing to Lee and Dan all the anguish she had suffered, she asked rhetorically, "What do you say?"

On Thursday, April 6, Lee and Dan tuned in to *L.A. Law*, one of Lee's favorite TV shows. A plot line in the previous weeks had been that the married couple in the Los Angeles law firm, played by Jill Eikenberry and Michael Tucker (the Stones referred to them as Jill and Michael), had adopted a baby through an open process. In the April 6 episode, the birth mother showed up at the lawyers' office unexpectedly, three months after signing the adoption papers. Jill and Michael acted pleased to see her and told her how much they felt like the baby's parents. "She knows who her mamma and dadda are," Michael happily reported. As the Stones summarized the episode, the birth mother replied, "You don't understand. I'm her mother. You'll *never* be her parents. I'm taking her back."

The show upset Lee and Dan profoundly. It was one more on the list of spectacles treating birth mothers as victims, open adoption as doomed, and adoption in general as an exploitative, murky enterprise. They stayed awake late, talking about the episode. At 12:30 a.m. the same night, Tom called them. "I have very bad news," he said. "Peggy told her parents about Rebecca, she's run away, and she's pregnant. Some heat's going to come your way." Tom passed on an assortment of other, sometimes alarming news bulletins: that Peggy had actually taken birth-control pills through the first four months of her pregnancy with Rebecca; that Peggy had become pregnant again not long before the Boston visit and was pregnant while she and Tom were in Boston; that Peggy had made lunch for Tom that afternoon and hadn't said a word about leaving.

After lunch, Tom later said, he had gone back to work and then out to dinner. He had tried to call Peggy but couldn't reach her, and soon after, at the restaurant, got a call from his roommate saying that Peggy's mother had phoned their apartment and sounded very worried. Tom went to the Basses' and learned that Peggy had left three notes: one for her roommates, apologizing about leaving town with the rent money that she had previously said she was trying to pay the landlord, as she was expected to, and saying that her parents would cover it; a second for Tom, saying she couldn't go on like this and that nothing seemed real; and a third for her parents, saying that a terrible thing had happened and that she and Tom were keeping it from them. Mrs. Bass asked Tom, "Did you and Peggy have a child?" Tom sketched their story, and Mr. Bass gave him an intense tongue-lashing. Peggy's roommates were at the Basses', too, and after a while Tom left with them for the train station, to see if they could find any clues to where Peggy might have gone. They didn't. Tom eventually called the Stones.

Half an hour later, at 1 a.m., Peggy's mother phoned the Stones. "I know that you have my granddaughter," she said. In tones they heard as all but threatening, she said she hoped that they were "fine" people who would "love Rebecca the way she deserved." She related that Peggy had spent the morning with her, planning a big family meal for the next night; that Peggy had been hoarding money for months—the rent money, a sizable sum that her parents had given her to pay for college tuition (which she apparently hadn't paid), and her earnings from working full-time (she had not been in school, despite what she had told Dan and Lee); and that Peggy had left her a letter telling her all about Rebecca and the adoption.

Peggy's mother admitted that Peggy had said she loved Lee and Dan, believed they were wonderful parents for Rebecca, and that Peggy didn't want Rebecca back. But, from talking with Tom and Mrs. Bass, the Stones got the impression that Peggy was distraught, particularly about Rebecca's adoption, and that, sometime between two and five o'clock on Thursday, she had walked away from her regular life. The fact that most disturbed them was that Peggy had been living a triple life: on top of the secrecy about the adoption that she had maintained with her parents, she had apparently not told them or the Stones the truth even about the parts of her life that had nothing to do with the adoption.

Dan had an independent piece of evidence that Peggy had been deceitful about more than the adoption. The week after Peggy visited Boston, when she was preoccupied by the rent, she had called Dan for advice. She told him a different version of the rent story. For Dan's ears, the problem was that a roommate was in charge of making the monthly payments and hadn't done so for three months. The delinquent party was off for a few days in New York City, and the landlord was demanding to pick up a check for $1,800 immediately from Peggy and threatening to have the roommates evicted. Peggy had asked Dan, Could the three of them be evicted? He had spent a morning on the phone trying to find legal advice for her. In retrospect, if her mother's version of events was correct, the question she had wanted an answer to must have been: If I take off with the rent money, will my roommates be evicted?

Lee was disturbed to hear that Peggy might have taken birth-control pills during her pregnancy with Rebecca, since that could have left the baby with a severe handicap, and she was angry at Tom for his ominous announcement of this ambiguous "fact." More critically, Lee feared from talking with him that she and Dan were about to lose their baby, as Jill and Michael had just done on *L.A. Law.* For the next couple of days, Lee suffered greatly: a chronic back pain reappeared, she became overvigilant in her supervision of Rebecca, and whenever she picked up the baby, she also imagined losing her.

The night before Tom's call, Peggy and Lee had spoken for about twenty minutes by phone. Peggy had complained that Tom was in a sour mood and that they were thinking of getting some counseling to see if they could "get some romance back into their relationship." The main purpose of the call was to make plans for meeting again with the Stones and Rebecca the following weekend in Washington. With hundreds of thousands of others, the Stones planned a trip to take part in a pro-choice abortion march on April 9. (Peggy had not made clear whether she would join the Stones on the march: without meaning to criticize their pro-choice stance, she had said that abortion "wasn't for her"; more than once, she had mistakenly referred to the event as a "right-to-life" march.) Even after the calls from Tom and Mrs. Bass, they kept their plan, but over the weekend they talked regularly about Peggy's disappearance. They said they were embarrassed about becoming "adoption bores." They wondered why Peggy and Tom hadn't told them she had got pregnant, if she had, and, overlooking the unwritten rule about taboo subjects they all had observed, why she hadn't talked more with them about how upset she was by Rebecca's adoption. Lee decided that until the adoption was approved by a judge, she didn't want any more contact with Peggy and Tom. The situation was too changeable and frightening.

On Monday night, back in Boston, Dan spoke with both Tom's mother and Peggy's. Peggy was back. She had gone to Orlando, Florida, for two days. Peggy wanted to make sure that the adoption was still "open"—that she could stay in contact with Dan, Lee, and Rebecca. Speaking for herself as well as Peggy, apparently, Mrs. Bass said the pictures that Lee and Dan had been sending of Rebecca "were driving the kids crazy," that it would be best if they stopped sending them, and that Peggy didn't want any contact with Lee and Dan for a while. Talking about Rebecca with Lee and Dan was making it hard for Peggy and Tom to put the whole thing behind them. From the mothers' descriptions, Peggy and Tom sounded so different from the people Lee and Dan knew that it was as if they had been "reprogrammed," the Stones said. Dan told Mrs. Bass and Mrs. Spaeth that he and Lee were happy to know Peggy was back and safe and that they were glad the secret was out, so Peggy and Tom could have the support of their families. With Mrs. Bass, he agreed that they would not be in touch with Peggy until she got in touch with them.

Two days later, Paul Dubroff reached Lee at home in midafternoon to say that he'd heard from "Tom's lawyer" and that a state administrator had also called him after hearing from a lawyer. Each wanted to know whether an interstate-transfer paper, which would have been required if Rebecca had been born in Delaware and moved to Massachusetts for adoption, had been signed. The paper was not relevant to Rebecca's adoption, since she had been born in Boston, but talking with Dubroff, Lee learned that the Jewish Family Service had been slow to take steps toward making the adoption final under Massachusetts law.

When Dan came home, he made some calls and discovered that the inquiries from Tom's lawyer had been placed the week before, when they were in Washington, to both Dubroff and the state administrator. Instead of being new links in a chain of escalating troubles, they were old news. The Stones were relieved. The following night, Dan phoned Tom. They spoke for an hour. About halfway through, Dan raised the subject of the call from the Jewish Family Service. He asked, "What's going on?" Tom said there was no lawyer on retainer; his parents had just wanted to know the legal status of Rebecca's adoption. Tom reported that he and Peggy had broken up, that Peggy was moving home from her townhouse, and that his main dealings with her were now about returning the keys to each other's places. He had grown tired of living behind a shroud of fiction (like the relaxed and happy adoption story that Peggy made up about the months before she got in touch with the Stones, instead of the truth about their difficult decision not to get married seven months into the pregnancy, Tom said); Tom felt relieved to have their secret in the open. Tom also told Dan that before Peggy went to Florida she had said she had her recent pregnancy aborted, but Tom was no longer certain what to believe. Tom was at loose ends. "I have so many kinds of grief going on, I need a Day-Timer to keep track of them," he said.

Dan and Lee felt in danger. "This whole last part of the experience—I feel on much shakier ground here," Dan said soon after. "Before, I was concerned about our relationship to Peggy and Tom. Now I'm concerned about something much bigger, which is Rebecca."

Abortion and Adoption

In his first Presidential Address to a joint session of Congress, in February of 1989, George Bush endorsed adoption with zest and a kind of innocence. "And for those children who are unwanted or abused or whose parents are deceased, we should encourage adoption," the President declared. "Let's make it easier for these kids to have parents who love them." Although brief, the mention took adoption beyond the tabloids ("Boy George To Adopt A Baby," the *Star* announced that week) and into the highest circles of respectability. Not long after that, Barbara Bush accepted an invitation to become the honorary chair of the National Committee For Adoption.

On one level, adoption warrants the enthusiasm of the Bush Administration, and of President and Mrs. Bush, who have adopted grandchildren, as much as does any current way of forming an American family. No other prospective parents besides adoptive parents are required to prove their fitness and, in effect, to be licensed for the job—a requirement that some see as an unwarranted intrusion. A remarkable fact, reported by Sandra Scarr, a professor of psychology at the University of Virginia who specializes in adoption, is that families with unrelated adopted children seem to reflect the traditional American model (husband, wife, and children, intact) more often than do biological families and to have more often withstood the stresses that cause the breakdown of families. However, families formed through the adoption of unrelated children are now less common than families formed through the divorce and remarriage of people with children. Of the 104,000 or so children adopted in 1986, the last year for which an estimate is available, more than half were adopted by stepparents or relatives.

On another level, however, the President's endorsement of adoption, in a slogan rather than a program, glosses over the complexity of the situation. "The American people know my position on right-to-life, favoring adoption over abortion," George Bush has often declared. To anoint adoption as the alternative to abortion is to link federal policy about the former with the almost fanatical politics surrounding the latter. Before the United States Supreme Court's July 1989 decision in *Webster v. Reproductive Health Services*, abortion was already "the most politically divisive legal issue of our time," as Justice Harry Blackmun wrote in his dissent in that case. After the Supreme Court's five-to-four decision in *Webster* allowing states to restrict the right to abortion and, in effect, inviting states to regulate abortion closely, the struggle instantly became even more combative. While the ultimate decision by a birth mother to place a child for adoption occurs after she rules out abortion, it is a denial of the large differences between the consequences of those choices to claim that, in given circumstances, adoption should or will generally follow from a no-abortion decision: many women, having rejected abortion, ultimately opt for single parenthood in poverty, for example. Decisions about abortion and adoption are likely to be made more clearly if they aren't artificially linked too tightly as alternatives.

The President's slogan also omits mention of an important third option: birth control. For teenagers, the rate of sexual activity in the United States and in other industrialized Western countries is approximately the same, but, with the rates of pregnancy and abortion much higher here, the use of birth control seems to be much lower. Nine out of ten pregnancies among unmarried teenagers are unintended; four out of ten teenage American girls become pregnant by the time they are twenty. Birth control is the least expensive, best timed, and most sensible step to take to avoid an unwanted pregnancy, aside from total abstention, which is an unlikely choice for the majority of Americans, since seven out of ten American girls and eight of ten boys now have sex while they are teenagers. As a matter of politics, emphasizing this option is dicey, for the Catholic Church and some other groups whose members oppose the right to abortion disapprove of the use of birth control as well.

Part of the appeal of the President's yoking of abortion and adoption is that it can be summarized on a bumper sticker. "Adoption, Not Abortion" seems to affirm life over loss, to offer homes to otherwise phantom children, and to fulfill the dreams of frustrated childless couples rather than leaving them wanting. The last point seems especially sound, given the profile of the American woman most likely to have an abortion: according to the Alan Guttmacher Institute, a research group focusing on reproductive health and family planning, she is likely to be unmarried, white, Protestant, and between twenty- and twenty-four, living in a metropolitan area, and earning anywhere from $11,000 on up (the rate of pregnancy among nonwhites is twice that of whites, but whites make up a much higher percentage of the total population). She matches the "ideal birth mother" description of many couples currently seeking to adopt.

For adoptees and adoptive parents, the abortion debate is particularly charged: decisions by women and their doctors to abort could have deprived adoptees of life and adoptive parents of children; happy adoptive families who think about the question can only be thankful for a birth mother's decision not to abort. But some facts suggest that the decision to have an abortion remains very personal and unusually resistant to any philosophical or religious command: sixteen percent of women who have abortions describe themselves as born-again or evangelical Christians, even though the leaders of those movements are persistent critics of abortion; and one-third of the women who have abortions are Catholic and are therefore acting against the dictates of their church. The President's approval of adoption may help persuade some women not to have an abortion, but it seems likely that in many cases his public exhortation won't overcome strong contrary private feelings. The relative constancy in the number of abortions and domestic adoptions of unrelated children during the past decade suggests that, for now at least, the National Abortion Rights Action League's broad pro-choice position, which can be summed up as "Abortion *and* Adoption," is an accurate description of options valued by women—putting aside its desirability as a statement of policy.

The Bush Administration has taken no position on conventional versus open adoption, reasoning that the choice is best made by agencies and prospective birth and adoptive parents. But another risk of linking abortion and adoption in the public mind is that the either/or position of the pro-life and pro-choice movements (or the anti-abortion and pro-abortion movements, as they regard each other) may reinforce the tendency in the adoption world to view conventional and open adoption as similarly irreconcilable, even if only as a result of an unwitting alignment. The Bush Administration, with its pro-life position, is now allied with the organization most closely identified with conventional adoption—for example, through the First Lady's role as honorary chair of the National Committee For Adoption. The alliance may strengthen another battle line where it need not have been drawn in the first place.

Even if one believes that the decision to abort or not should not be left to the individual, choice in adoption (whether conventional, semi-open, open, or cooperative adoption) is a different matter. It seems much easier to justify allowing all kinds of adoption and difficult to rationalize prohibiting any one kind, as some advocates of open and conventional adoption propose about the other. The best available evidence indicates that it is possible to have successful adoptions of each type. Despite the vigor of advocacy for and against open and conventional adoption especially, the distinctiveness of each individual adoption and the inconclusiveness of the evidence about the advantages and disadvantages of each type support the judgment that policies favoring one form of adoption over the others, or prohibiting certain forms, would be a mistake.

The National Committee For Adoption takes neither a pro-choice nor a pro-life position on abortion, although its work with pro-life leaders such as the Reverend Jerry Falwell in a joint effort to rebuild this country's maternity homes has led some of the Committee's critics in the open-adoption movement to view that neutral position as an expedient pose. In any event, the Committee makes a good case that a shift to the adoption category both of a small fraction of the pregnancies included in the number of abortions in this country (1,588,550 in 1986) and of those included in the number of births to unmarried women (878,477, over half to teenagers) would result in a large increase in the proportion of unrelated domestic infant adoptions (24,589).

Two lines of reasoning suggest that the equation is not that simple. The first, offered by Reuben Pannor, argues that the current American adoption system would have difficulty in handling significantly more adoptions and that a big jump in the numbers of babies available for adoption could lead to the export of American babies to other countries, in contrast with the current movement of children mostly in the other direction, with Americans now adopting approximately ten thousand children from abroad each year (almost thirty percent of all the unrelated infant adoptions in this country).

The second, and more compelling, argument is that many unmarried mothers end up keeping their babies and that often those who follow this path confront serious problems. They are far less likely to finish high school or, for that matter, to get married; they are far more likely to be poor and receive public assistance; the development of their children, as a result of these hardships, is more likely to suffer. One alternative for relieving the pressures on these young women and their children would be for the government to go beyond the recently proposed and substantial day-care funding for poor children, to provide a guaranteed minimum amount of child support which in effect would compensate children for the loss of one parent and allow single parents to spend at least some time with their very young children. In other industrialized countries, some such support has long been in place.

This sort of additional subsidy seems unlikely to win government backing. Aside from it, a program that, on the one hand, recognizes a woman's manifest choice to abort a pregnancy or carry the fetus to term and raise the child and that, on the other hand, encourages more pregnant single women to consider placing their children for adoption—especially those at social and economic risk—seems to deserve serious attention. A generation ago, four out of five unmarried new mothers chose such a placement. By 1986, the number had fallen to one out of twenty-five: whereas almost ninety-five percent of the birth mothers in unrelated infant adoptions are unmarried, roughly the same percentage of unmarried mothers now keep their babies. (One of every hundred single black birth mothers placed her child for adoption; one of eight single white birth mothers did.)

Of the almost nine million American families headed by a single parent, the vast majority are headed by women. The scandal that fifteen percent of all American children are poor is overshadowed by the fact that four times that number— almost sixty percent—of children living with a single parent are in poverty. Many of the parents handing down this legacy of hardship are teenagers (more than half of all welfare payments, almost twenty billion dollars in 1987, now go to women who gave birth as teenagers), whose million or so pregnancies a year constitute what some health experts call an epidemic. If only two out of twenty-five of these young women had decided to place their babies for adoption rather than keep them, a resonant economic and social problem would have been eased.

Some women who might be included in the hardship statistics choose not to be. For now, women in poor families have abortions at a higher rate than women who are better off: the abortion rate of women covered by Medicaid is about three times that for women not covered. Pro-life activists regard these numbers as evidence that poor women use abortion as a form of birth control. Pro-choice activists cite them as an indication of the class of women most likely to be affected by new restrictions on abortion as a result of the Supreme Court's *Webster* decision and, in its wake, the likely prohibition of abortions in some public hospitals, the likelihood of new restrictions on abortions for teenagers, and the possible outlawing of abortion even in some cases of rape or incest. If it is unacceptable, as the Bush Administration holds, to try to relieve the problem by counseling more young women to consider abortion rather than giving birth to children who are likely to suffer economically and otherwise, it should be a priority to offer both the mothers and the children a way out of the cycle of hardship. One route is through adoption.

America's Waiting Children, a report submitted in March of 1988 to President Ronald Reagan by a government task force on adoption led by Mary Sheila Gall, encouraged such an effort. Gall was once Vice-President Bush's deputy on domestic policy and is now his Administration's chief adviser on adoption in her position as Assistant Secretary of Health and Human Services. The report contains a mixed bag of recommendations. It summarizes overdue general reforms (treating adoptive children the same as biological children for purposes of Social Security, disability, and retirement benefits; asking insurance companies to cover the births of adoptive and biological children identically; and asking employers to give new adoptive parents the same amount of leave as they do biological parents). It describes some of the new complexities in the adoption world (in forty states, biological fathers are now given the opportunity to oppose an adoption or to try to gain custody of the child, even if they have no emotional ties to the mother). In line with its main purpose, it promotes more flexibility in the adoption system (by encouraging adoption of children with special needs by adults in their forties and fifties, by people with handicaps, and, with the specific and sharply debated exception of homosexuals, by other parents who might be considered unconventional).

The report, however, sidestepped what seem to be the essentials of the single-mother problem: that single mothers and children are likely to fare better economically if they do not remain together; that a sizable portion of the children who initially remain with their single mothers are likely to end up in foster care (of the 276,000 or so children in foster care, half were born out of wedlock); and that, until the system is improved, mothers who are eventually going to place their children for adoption can increase their chances of a successful adoption if they face the choice at birth and make an early placement. (Joyce Ladner, professor of social work at Howard University, has made a similar point in recommending the revival of orphanages, on grounds that many children in foster care would fare better if they were "permanently and quickly" separated from their biological parents.) If the last observation seems callous, it is in part a reflection of the marginal standing that adoption has among the options available to pregnant young women.

An Adoption Working Group in the Bush Administration is now directly addressing some of the problems that burden the foster-care system. Its focus is on families at risk, where financial stress and drug use lead to considerably more violent treatment of children today than a generation ago, and where crack babies, infants with AIDS, and abused children are common. In June of 1989, there were 20,000 foster-care children who had been matched for adoption and were waiting legal approval; 16,000 more were ready for adoption but had not yet been placed. The goal of the Administration is to increase those numbers by raising the general level of foster care, improving counseling for families, reuniting children with families as soon as possible and, where that is not possible, speeding "permanency planning"—helping families develop plans for adoption, and keeping children from enduring years of "foster-care drift."

To induce more families to adopt children with special needs, a description that applies to many children in foster care, the President in 1989 proposed a tax deduction of three thousand dollars for families who make such adoptions. The federal government already gives financial aid to children in foster care whose biological families are poor enough to qualify for welfare. When these foster children are adopted, no matter what the income of their adoptive parents, the adoptive families receive a payment on behalf of the child until the child reaches age eighteen.

The number of children in foster care and the widely acknowledged strains on the system suggest that adoption can't be divorced from other social issues. Adoption has usually satisfied a need rather than being an end in itself, and matching foster children with would-be parents fits the pattern. It is perhaps today's orphan train. But viewing adoption as a heroic arm outstretched to foster children, as George Bush has sometimes suggested—most significantly in a July 1989 memorandum to the heads of all departments in the federal government, stating the Administration's support for the "Adoption Option," and in a November 1989 Thanksgiving proclamation of National Adoption Week—overstates the ability of adoption to solve the large problem being addressed.

A more realistic appraisal is that the "waiting children" the President has set his sights on are less a problem that can be solved by adoption than they are a window on the current state of America's underclass, whose plight sharply worsened in the Reagan years. Nicholas Lemann observed recently in *The Atlantic Monthly* that "most experts have been edging cautiously toward the idea that some women have babies out of wedlock, get on welfare, and essentially drop out of the economy for long periods of time." For these women this is a rational choice, some experts now contend, because the welfare system offers reliable support that the economy does not. For society it is very costly. Seen in relation to the problems of welfare, and of foster care as a facet of those, adoption appears to offer only modest help. It is an apt expression of the Bush belief in a thousand points of light (widespread individual good works), when the challenge at hand demands a far more intensive social commitment.

Family

Since the publication in 1929 of the anthropologist Raymond Firth's study of adoption among the Maori people, in New Zealand, research about adoption on the islands and atolls of Oceania, 2,500 miles to the southwest of Hawaii, in the Pacific Ocean, has yielded a variety of reports about systems that contrast with our own. On the Namoluk Atoll, in the Caroline Islands, adoption has been an economic equalizer, a means to distribute among relatives one of that tiny land's precious resources, its children. On the Manihi Atoll, in the Tuamotu Archipelago, not far from Tahiti, twenty-five percent of the two hundred or so residents were at one time adopted, most by blood relatives. The reasons for those adoptions ranged from giving a childless couple the chance to have a family, to easing the burden on a large household, to providing children who could care for adoptive parents as they aged, to giving an older couple the chance to have a child in the house once again. Adoption has meant that, in the harsh conditions of the island, a child could lose the adults who gave birth to him but their roles were almost always filled immediately by others.

On the main Tongan island, Tongatapu, east of the Fiji Islands, adoption is a high honor. Frequently, adoptees are the favorite children of their adoptive parents, and adoption has increased the adoptees' opportunities for kinship and access to valuable resources like land. Among the Marshallese, on the Arno Atoll in the Marshall Islands, teachers have adopted students to show deep appreciation ("adoption in the afternoon"); friends have adopted friends, who become a kind of sibling; young people have adopted older people to repay a debt of gratitude; and couples have adopted children, in the more usual arrangement. Biological parents have revoked the adoption of their biological child when they felt the adoptive parents were not feeding him well or not bringing him up properly. Years ago, in the Gilbert Islands, immediately to the southeast, almost every child was adopted at birth, with the exception of the children of poor people, who, according to the anthropologist Robert Briffault, "may [have] suffer[ed] the mortification of having to bring up their own children."

Advocates of open adoption cite the adoptions of Oceania— where the communities are small and adoptees know their biological families and tend to add to their circles of kinship rather than substituting one for another—as proof that the model is well established and not the radical innovation it is sometimes made out to be. Yet the societies of that region are so different from our own that the example probably serves better as a reminder of how varied cultural practices can be, rather than as a precedent for American adoption.

Still, the Oceania studies, focusing on the general purpose of adoption there to create new and reinforce old ties of kinship and spur the sharing of resources, to foster alliances, and to contribute to the survival of the population, suggest the good sense of considering adoption in the United States from the same dispassionate point of view as the studies do. During the 1988 Presidential campaign, George Bush defined the context: "I am a man who knows in his heart that it all comes to family—that all our best endeavors come back to that core." Even as the makeup of American families is in flux (three out of five women with children have jobs outside the home, six out of ten children are likely to live with a single parent at some point before they are eighteen), the traditional image of the family remains powerful, in part because families at their best can provide so much: nurture, stability, economic support, opportunity, and a sense of belonging. Above all, American adoption must be seen as an institution for creating and expanding families.

A decade from now, after commentary has had a chance to catch up with innovations in society, adoption may seem a simple matter to assess. The challenging subjects are more apt to be techniques such as fetal adoption, in which a fetus is removed from the original mother and transplanted to, and carried to term in, either the adoptive mother or an incubator similar to those now used to care for babies born prematurely. Attention to the difficult question of who is a "parent" (a donor of genes? a gestator? a committed caretaker?) will likely suggest how much more confusing the larger one about the definition of a family will be, as well.

But even then, as now in the case of adoption, the sense of belonging, of feeling a deep and abiding connection, will go a long way toward defining a family and make otherwise bedrock factors like economic support seem secondary. In our present psychologically attuned culture, that sense of belonging is a bond, a shadow, and a kind of wound, an anchor, a looking glass, and a home. Once adoption has been accepted as a means of creating a family, and, with it, the idea that biology is not the only door into a family, then the potential for families of different types seems capable of great expansion. They can be created through special-needs adoptions, transracial adoptions, international adoptions, and so on, as well as through adoptions by unconventional parents. Rather than being a "second class" institution, which is how Elizabeth Bartholet, a professor at Harvard Law School, has described American law's pigeonholing of adoption, it can be seen to have its own strengths. In that light, conventional and open adoption become flip sides of a single coin. They are both oriented to the biological family as the ideal (conventional adoption by imitation, open adoption by deference to genetic heritage), and seem to be limited visions of what adoption can offer.

The concern that lingers even for enthusiasts of new visions stems from a perplexing question in any form of parenthood—the effect nurture has on nature. Adults contemplating adoption ask whether they can make a difference in what kind of person a child turns out to be. Since 1875, when Sir Francis Galton, who was a cousin of Darwin, invented "the Twin Method," studies of adoptees and of twins have been primary tools in the attempt to measure how nature and nurture each contributes to human development. The pendulum of opinion has swung between the extremes of belief in omnipotent genes, at the turn of the century, and of total faith in environmentalism (the impact of parents, families, schools, and the like), in the years following the Second World War. In 1979, the Minnesota Study of Twins Reared Apart, directed by Thomas J. Bouchard, began to look at adopted twins, in the field's most comprehensive recent inquiry. "The evidence supporting the existence of genetic influences upon human cognitive abilities is overwhelming," Bouchard and a colleague observed. At least half the variation in I.Q. is attributable to genetic differences, they found; about thirty percent is linked to family characteristics such as social and economic status, and about twenty percent is due to factors not shared with anyone else in the family, such as order of birth in the family.

Apart from the influence of genetics on "special mental abilities" (spatial perception, verbal ability, and perceptual speed and accuracy), a perhaps more surprising contention of the Minnesota team is that genes appear to influence human behavior and personality as much as do environmental factors. The "Jim twins," a set of identical twins named Jim Lewis and Jim Springer, who were adopted by different families in Ohio at four weeks of age, suffered similar migraine headaches at the same age. Identical twins reared separately by a Jewish father in Trinidad and a Catholic mother in Germany scored almost identically on a three-hundred-item personality test called the Multidimensional Personality Questionnaire, which measures eleven traits, from social potency (such as forcefulness) and well-being (cheerfulness or gloom) to the need of those being tested for control.

From one point of view, these findings seem to transform the nature-nurture dichotomy into a victory of determinism over free will. Leon Kamin, a psychologist at Northeastern University, commented: "The genetic interpretation is getting a much warmer reception now than it would have gotten twenty or thirty years ago, because it suits the temper of the times. If you decide that social problems like poverty and crime are genetic, you don't have to try to do anything about them—people want to forget that there's an environmental influence on behavior as well."

In the adoption world, the Minnesota findings concerning genetic influence have strengthened the hand of open-adoption advocates, by underscoring the benefits to an adoptee and to adoptive parents of knowing the birth parents from whom the adoptee inherits his genes. The findings have led the proponents of conventional adoption to redefine it so that the birth parents are asked to provide the adoptive parents, and eventually the adoptee, with as much information as possible about their social and medical histories.

But the obvious interrelation of genetic and environmental influences on behavior, personality, achievement, and other expressions of development seems to make adoption more similar to than different from biological nurture. Sandra Scarr, professor of psychology at the University of Virginia, summarized: "From all of our research with adoptive families and biological families, it looks like the best environments provide opportunities for children to explore what they might turn out to be, but that, in any case, they turn out to be themselves."

Adoption's function of satisfying corresponding, and changing, social (and personal) needs suggests that the adoption world will be perennially unsettled, although outsiders may not notice: like other narrow, argumentative communities, it is preoccupied with its needs and hopes, and often is lost in the larger American crowd. Sandra Scarr says: "Among the traumas that most people face, including adoptees, being adopted is not high on the list." Many adoptive families are like Tolstoy's happy ones, quietly content. And, in some respects, the noisy part of that world has reached consensus about some issues that once divided it.

Few claim that birth mothers in the nineteen-forties, fifties, and sixties, who had no choice between raising their children and giving them up for adoption, were fairly treated. Almost no one contends that birth parents and adoptees who wish to seek each other out should be prevented by law from doing so, or from having the help, at some point, of any legal documents available from state or adoption agencies. The old debate about whether adoptees should be told that they are adopted has given way to the question of when and how to tell them. Adversaries in the ongoing debate concerning the best way to carry out an adoption concur that adoptions involve a triad of interests—those of the adoptee, those of the birth parents, and those of the adoptive parents, each of whom deserves respect from the other two and from the agencies, lawyers, and others who bring them together. These new compacts often give priority to the best interests of the child, which is what was supposed to distinguish American adoption from European adoption for almost a century and a half. Of all the issues involved in adoption, the question of how best to serve the interests of the child in adoptions of unrelated infants, which now represent perhaps a quarter of all legal adoptions in this country, remains most prominent. It frames the debate about how to define those interests with a tender gravity, and infant adoptions are seen by most students of the subject as the most likely to succeed.

Rebecca

In the months after Peggy told her parents about Rebecca's adoption, she cut off contact with everyone except her immediate family and a small circle of friends—Tom, the Stones, and the Roses in particular were cut off. Her mother told the Stones that Peggy considered open adoption "a nightmare." Her father said that "open adoption may be great for some people, but not for us." As Tom put it: "There was a lot of anger directed at Massachusetts and the Jewish Family Service." According to him, "the Basses felt that Peggy had been coerced, surrounded by adoptive parents, with no outside opinion given." Mr. Bass remarked: "We feel that the whole time in Boston she was misled and she was cajoled. When she was going through postpartum depression, she was forced to make decisions. Everyone knows how bad that is. We feel the whole situation was deceitful." He also said, "What's past is past," and indicated that they were all trying to put the experience behind them.

After Peggy returned from Florida, Tom said, he had about a half-dozen limited dealings with her. "She's usually wanted stuff back," he said wryly. She was in therapy, he reported.

Peggy asked Tom for items in his possession that might help her and her counselor. At her request, he had recently given her a blanket and a formula bottle of Rebecca's. Peggy was very businesslike ("She calls herself Margaret," Tom noted), and claimed she was doing great. "The first time everything was 'great,' it had only been four weeks" since she disappeared. Tom observed: "I certainly wasn't great." Tom speculated about why she had gone to Florida ("Maybe that was the last place that everything was cool before this happened," in the fall of 1987). He blamed himself for not having recognized how troubled Peggy was about the adoption. ("I thought I knew her better than anybody else. I didn't see it.") He felt conned by her.

In mid-June of 1989, Tom remarked: "I feel good about Dan and Lee, and the adoption, the way it progressed." Then, referring to the events of the previous few months, he said: "I feel terrible about all this. I'm sure Dan and Lee didn't sign on for this sort of drama." He went on: "I have kept in touch. I like them. But I've decided I'm going to have to back off. At first, my family was all 'We're going to have to get the baby back.' Now they're resigned to the fact that she's a bi- ological relation but not a family member. Peggy and I picked Dan and Lee, and we might as well let them do what we picked them to do. The other thing I've been doing is trying to take care of myself: just work and live. Every day is dif- ferent, and maybe one day it will be different enough so I won't have to deal with this stuff. It was going to happen either way, but it's too bad it blew up in a crisis. This is just my point of view, of course. Peggy's is different, and I have no idea what she'd say."

At the end of June, I received a note in Peggy's handwriting, in response to a letter from me, acknowledging that there were "some discrepancies" between what she had previously re- ported about her part in the adoption and what had actually occurred. Her "story was not based on reality" and was "in- correct factually," the note said. "I am now in a different place

emotionally thru counseling and realize I should not have contributed to the story."

On May 26, 1989, almost a year after Peggy had first called
Lee, the Stones went with Rebecca, the Roses, and some other
friends to probate court, in the Old Courthouse in downtown
Boston. A hearing on the legal status of Rebecca's adoption
had been scheduled, and according to the Stones' lawyer, the
hearing was a formality: the adoption was definitely going to
be approved. That morning, Lee had said to Dan, "So this is
it, right?"

Dan felt superstitious. "I'm not saying anything," he said.

Lee insisted, "Is it going to happen today? We'll be safe
after?"

Dan answered, "No. You can't say that."

The courtroom was crowded with people who had appoint-
ments before the judge: relatives contesting wills; men and
women in the process of divorce; children waiting to be placed
in foster homes. The judge was a rosy-cheeked Irishwoman
in her late fifties. Rather than taking the Stones into her cham-
bers for a private hearing as sometimes happens with adoptions, she asked them to approach the bench with Rebecca,
in open court.

The judge said, "I want to congratulate you. I've approved
your papers. This is the nicest thing I get to do all day, and
I hope you continue to be as happy as you are today." The
judge held Rebecca on her lap for photographs, and when the
baby tried to pull a blotter off the bench, the courtroom burst
into laughter. From the periphery, there seemed to be no
stiffness or formality. The entire proceeding, including the
approach to the bench and the walk away from it, took two
minutes.

Dan commented: "We were trying not to make the legal
event too significant, wanting our feelings about Rebecca to
be primary, but it was. It was a formal acknowledgment of
our bond. It made us feel technically more secure."

Lee: "When the papers were signed, I felt protected. I felt, *Finally*."

Lee (June of 1989): "I oftentimes feel I understand what's going on with Peggy, and can imagine what it would be like to give birth to Rebecca, to leave her with us, to see her that once, to break up with my boyfriend, and then to be reprogrammed by my parents. Mostly, I feel very sympathetic, but I also feel very sad that she's cut out of our lives and I can't contact her again without her parents thinking I'm trying to stir something up. But part of me is angry, feeling betrayed, that she didn't say, 'I'm having a hard time,' because we were so open with each other and were so close, especially that last weekend in March. Why did she go on that way for so long? I feel angry at myself that I didn't tune in: it was too good to be true. I feel terrible about this. I don't know what to do. I feel like writing a short note saying, We're thinking of you. But I don't want to upset her if she needs some distance from us. Dan thinks she knows this. I'm wondering if she's angry at us: How could she not be? We have her biological baby. It was so strange, to have talked with her the night before and then she was gone.

"I really looked up to her: that she was so strong, to go through that whole summer, the birth and postpartum and after, without cracking. I still feel that way. But now she seems much younger.

"I would do an open adoption again, but I would not carry on the relationship after the birth. I would send pictures, maybe, or a letter after a year, and that's it. It's very important to have that control, and to know about the baby. It's still important to me.

"Tom has been lovely. On Mother's Day, he left a message on our answering machine. His voice is a little shaky, and it always makes me think he's about to reclaim Rebecca, because of that waver. He said, 'Lee, I just want to wish you a happy Mother's Day. I can't imagine anyone being a more wonderful mother for Rebecca. I hope you're having a nice day.' He asked for two pictures: one we call Madonna and Child, of Peggy holding Rebecca. And the 'Give-her-to-me!' photo— with me watching Peggy with my hands on my hips and my elbows out, and Peggy holding Rebecca."

Dan: "I think that the situation had been set up in such a way that Peggy was leading two lives. There was her family life and her life around having made this decision: I think our coming to Washington prompted the realization that it was impossible to keep them separate: us; Rebecca; her family. We were all going to be very close. Our relationship and her eagerness to share everything with us brought this to a head and made her realize how untenable the situation was. And as she was moving away from Tom, she needed her family; one displaced the other. I think she wanted everything to be a certain way, and it couldn't any longer. At the beginning, when we first talked, she would say she didn't want to tell her parents, because they would offer to raise the baby and she knew that wasn't right. She needed to do things in her own way. And now she's doing the same thing in reverse. She's keeping us away, in the aftermath; they're both all or nothing. She had a commitment to making sure Rebecca would be all right. That was what she always said. That she wanted to see the baby through. When she came and saw everything was O.K., the trappings of the relationship started to fall away, and she picked up her regular life.

"I write letters to her in my head, letting her know she can do whatever she wants to, that Rebecca is doing O.K., and that the door is open to her. She must have kept a lot inside, and she's doing what she needs to, to heal. Everyone in Boston who met her wondered about that: she's such a powerful person that we all decided not to press her to do what she didn't seem to want to at the time, and force her to face what she wasn't. I always felt that it wasn't appropriate for us to make her grapple with her pain, just as it felt wrong to share what it felt like to be infertile. I don't have access to Peggy's thoughts

now. Suddenly, I imagine, she had this overwhelming sense
of loss.

"I think that the Basses feel that we had a blithe, unin-
formed, and superficial view of the depth of their daughter's
feelings. That we think open adoption is simple and wonderful
and everyone should try it, and don't recognize their daughter's struggle and pain. I can understand why they could think
that, and don't quite know what to do with it.

"I feel very fortunate to have had as intimate an experience
with Rebecca's birth mom and dad as we've had. I feel I know
something about Rebecca that I couldn't otherwise. We have
the incredible pleasure of talking about her birth, which Lee
and I do a lot, to have been there at that event, and to know
something intimate about her ancestry. The experience with
Peggy and Tom was very intense, if brief.

"But with that pleasure comes a knowledge of the pain. I
can conjure up an image of them, and identify with them, in
a way that is very personal, complicated, and sad. I don't
know what the implications of that are for the future."

At ten months, Rebecca was a happy, energetic baby. She
had a full head of curly red hair and a gummy smile uninter-
rupted by teeth. She liked to babble and scoot on her hands
and knees, and when Lee and Dan kissed her neck, they were
invariably rewarded with a giggle.

"Morning is an especially wonderful time," Lee said. "She
pals around with us a lot while we're doing stuff in preparation
for moving, which we're about to do, and Rebecca and I were
at the bakery the other day with Dan. She was sparky, ornery,
and really expressive, and I had this surge of well-being about
us as a happy unit. The first few months with her were hard
for me, because I hadn't resolved the infertility stuff and I felt
shadowed by that August weekend with Peggy and Tom. But
that has become hazy. Now we have this wonderful little
family. In the morning, we run up and down the hall together.

I make coffee. Rebecca loves to sit in her high chair and feed herself finger food. She's very social and extroverted, putting her hand out in this funny Lady Di wave and wrinkling her nose. By this time, I'm totally taken with her. I know it's going to get complicated. She's so assertive. But it's very nice to see the three of us as buddies. It's such a cliché, but I don't think of her as adopted."

Acknowledgments

Many people helped me during the time I spent on this book. I would like to thank some, in particular, who don't necessarily share my views: Annette Baran and Reuben Pannor, of Los Angeles, California; Elizabeth Bartholet, of the Harvard Law School, in Cambridge, Massachusetts; Thomas J. Bouchard, Jr., of the University of Minnesota, in Minneapolis; Paul Dubroff, Elayna Kirschtel, and Shirley Silver, of the Jewish Family Service of Greater Framingham, in Framingham, Massachusetts; Carol Gustavson, of Adoptive Parents for Open Records, in Long Valley, New Jersey; Janet L. Hookailo, of the Office for Children, the Commonwealth of Massachusetts, in Boston; Ruth Hubbell, of the National Adoption Information Clearinghouse, in Washington, D.C.; Vicki Jackson, of the Georgetown University Law Center, in Washington, D.C.; Joyce Johnson and Beverly Jones, of the Child Welfare League of America, in Washington, D.C.; Sharon Kaplan, of Parenting Resources, in Tustin, California; Mabel Leed, of the Children's Aid Society, in New York City; Ruth G. McRoy, of the University of Texas, in Austin; Diane Michelsen and Jennifer Lenox, of the law offices of Diane Michelsen, in Walnut Creek, California; Susan Miller-Havens, of Harvard University; Joyce Maguire Pavao, of the Family Center, in Somerville, Massachusetts; William Pierce, Jeffrey Rosenberg, and Mary Beth Seader, of the National Committee For Adoption, in Washington, D.C.; Roger Porter, Mary Gall, Emily Mead, and Betty J. Stewart, of the United States government, in Washington, D.C.; Kent Ravenscroft, of Georgetown University, in Washington, D.C.; Sandra Scarr, of the University of Virginia, in Charlottesville; Joe Soll, of the American Adoption Congress, in New York City; and Michael Sullivan, of the Southwest Adoption Center, in Scottsdale, Arizona.

At *The New Yorker*, Robert Gottlieb gave me the opportunity to try this project, and accepted it with an openness and intensity of interest that helped justify for me the long stretch when its outcome was uncertain; C. Patrick Crow gave me fine counsel as I worked on the project and skillfully edited my manuscript for the magazine. Anne Mortimer-Maddox was deft and diplomatic in checking facts, and made other elegant contributions. At important junctures, Martin Baron, Joseph Cooper, Bruce Diones, Ernie Fesler, Eleanor Gould, Martha Kaplan, Terry McGarry, Sheila McGrath, John Smith, Natasha Turi, Marcia Van Meter, and Joy Wiener eased my job by helping solve some nettlesome problems.

Linda Healey, of Farrar, Straus and Giroux, orchestrated the publication of this book in hardcover and contributed, in particular, by suggesting how to reshape the chapter on abortion and adoption; her assistant, Amy Peck, took care of a range of key details; Carmen Gomezplata, the firm's chief copy editor, improved the manuscript with her precise red pencil; and Helene Atwan and Bridget Marmion, who direct the firm's publicity and marketing departments, supported the book with energy and sophistication, as did Laurie Brown, Holly McGhee, and others at the firm.

Steven Lewers, Alan Andres, Chris Coffin, Becky Saikia-Wilson, Luise Erdmann and others oversaw the publication of this paperback for Houghton Mifflin. They won my gratitude by working expertly to polish the text and broaden the book's readership.

Rafe Sagalyn, my literary agent, expressed belief in the book before I thought my manuscript would become one. His colleagues, Lisa DiMona and Leigh Feldman, also cheered on the project. Schellie Hagan checked facts for the book and, with real facility, did a lot under pressure to help ensure its basic accuracy.

In this project especially, my sisters, Joanna and Margi Caplan, gave me extraordinary support, as did their husbands, Robert Blaemire and Phillip Bricker. David Ignatius, Robert Shapiro, and William Yeomans buoyed me with their friendship. So did Ellen Semonoff and Daniel Meltzer, who provided me with a home-away-from-home while I did some reporting. I would not have written about adoption if Richard and Ruth Rogers had not urged my wife and me to consider the option for ourselves; they played an essential part in our own adoption.

As with almost every piece of writing I have done for the past fifteen years, my wife, Susan, has been a clear-sighted, generous, and loving partner. This book is dedicated to her and our daughter.

Finally, I am grateful to the people I call Peggy Bass, Lee Duncan, Dan Stone, Tom Spaeth, and Jim and Dina Rose. They shared with me an intense, a surprising, and, I believe, an illuminating experience, and served as my guides through unusual emotional territory. They made it possible for me to write on a human scale about an issue of wide significance.

A Note on Sources

For anyone interested in other sources of information on adoption, I suggest the following:

SERVICE ORGANIZATIONS

American Adoption Congress
Cherokee Station
P.O. Box 20137
New York, New York 10028-0051

> *The Adoption Bibliography.* New York: American Adoption Congress, 1988.

Child Welfare League of America
440 First Street, N.W., Suite 310
Washington, D.C. 20001-2085

> Posner, Julia L., *CWLA's Guide to Adoption Agencies: A National Directory of Adoption Agencies and Adoption Resources.* Washington, D.C.: Child Welfare League of America, 1989.

National Committee For Adoption
1930 17th Street, N.W.
Washington, D.C. 20009

> *1989 Adoption Factbook.* Washington, D.C.: National Committee for Adoption.

CANADIAN INFORMATION

National Adoption Desk
Social Service Programs Branch
Health & Welfare Canada
Brooke Claxton Building
Ottawa, Ontario, Canada K1A 1B5

GENERAL BACKGROUND

Bolles, Edmund Blair, *The Penguin Adoption Handbook: A Guide to Creating Your New Family*. New York: Penguin Books, 1984.

Friedman, Rochelle, and Bonnie Gradstein, *Surviving Pregnancy Loss* (Section IV: "Planning for the Future"). Boston: Little, Brown, 1982.

Gilman, Lois, *The Adoption Resource Book*. New York: Harper & Row, 1984.

Lifton, Betty Jean, *Lost & Found: The Adoption Experience*. New York: Harper & Row, 1988.

Smith, Jerome, and Franklin I. Miroff, *You're Our Child: The Adoption Experience*. Lanham, Md.: Madison Books, 1987.

SPECIALIZED BACKGROUND

Benet, Mary Kathleen, *The Politics of Adoption*. New York: The Free Press, 1976.

Brady, Ivan, ed., *Transactions in Kinship: Adoption and Fosterage in Oceania*. Honolulu: University Press of Hawaii, 1976.

Bremner, Robert H., ed., *Children and Youth in America: A Documentary History*. Cambridge, Mass.: Harvard University Press, 1970.

Feigelman, William, and Arnold R. Silverman, *Chosen Children: New Patterns of Adoptive Relationships*. New York: Praeger, 1983.

Hill, Robert B., *Informal Adoption among Black Families*. Washington, D.C.: National Urban League, 1977.

Hollinger, Joan, ed., *Adoption Law & Practice*. New York: Matthew Bender & Company, 1988.

Kirk, H. David, *Shared Fate: A Theory of Adoption and Mental Health*. New York: The Free Press, 1964.

OPEN ADOPTION

Kaplan, Sharon, and Mary Jo Rillera, *Cooperative Adoption: A Handbook*. Westminster, Calif.: Triadoption Publications, 1985.

Lindsay, Jeanne Warren, *Open Adoption: A Caring Option*. Buena Park, Calif.: Morning Glory Press, 1988.

McRoy, Ruth G., Harold Grotevant, and Kerry White, *Openness in Adoption*. New York: Praeger, 1988.

Silber, Kathleen, and Phylis Speedlin, *Dear Birthmother*. Cape Coral, Fla.: The Adoption Awareness Press, 1983.

Sorosky, A. D., Annette Baran, and Reuben Pannor, *The Adoption Triangle: The Effects of the Sealed Record on Adoptees, Birth Parents, and Adoptive Parents*. New York: Anchor Press/ Doubleday, 1978.

The Search Movement

Fisher, Florence, *The Search for Anna Fisher*. New York: Arthur Fields Books, Inc., 1973.

Triseliotis, John, *In Search of Origins: The Experiences of Adopted People*. Boston: Beacon Press, 1973.

Transracial Adoption

Simon, Rita James, and Howard Alstein, *Transracial Adoption*. New York: John Wiley & Sons, 1977.

LINCOLN CAPLAN is a staff writer for *The New Yorker*. He is the author of *The Tenth Justice: The Solicitor General and the Rule of Law* and *The Insanity Defense and the Trial of John W. Hinckley, Jr.* Mr. Caplan was born in New Haven, Connecticut, in 1950, is a graduate of Harvard College and Harvard Law School, and has been a Guggenheim Fellow and a White House Fellow. He lives with his wife and daughter in Washington, D.C.